Praise of "Morph America - Peace Smarts" Team

"Thank you for the work you are doing for our children."

President Clinton

"I've watched you...You are doing a great job."
Oprah Winfrey

"Merrie Lynn Ross, it is an honor to present you with the 'Humanitarian Peace Award' for your dedication, visionary insight, and the hope you give parents and children to create a world of unity and peace. "

Four Worlds International

"Girl Scouts have benefited across the nation, learning ethical tools in the Peace Smarts curriculum. Merrie Lynn, unanimous kudos for your inspirational energy to help our families grow strong."

Sheila Lewis, Girl Scouts of America.

"Merrie Lynn your anti-bully project is needed in our schools and community. Keep the plan rolling forward."

Sheriff Lee Baca, Los Angeles County

Volume 1: Morphing Across Curriculum

Morphing

OF

AMERICA™

Merrie Way Community™
Los Angeles, CA

The Transformational Process 4 Youth
Grades 6-12

Merrie Lynn Ross
Gloria DeGaetano, M. Ed.

Morphing of America is dedicated to Mr. William Ellis

Bill never met a man, woman, or child who was not his friend.

His motto? "The best thing in life is giving."

Bill's generosity has made the Morphing of America project a reality...

a dream come true.

As an entrepreneur, a philanthropist, a brilliant mentor,

and a loving human being...

THANK YOU, BILL.

YOU GAVE US A JUMPSTART...

TO MORPH AMERICA.

MERRIE WAY COMMUNITY™

13601 Ventura Boulevard, Suite 227
Sherman Oaks, CA 91423
www.morphamerica.org

Cover illustration by Steve Rottblatt.
Typesetting & layout by H&H Design Company

Morphing of America

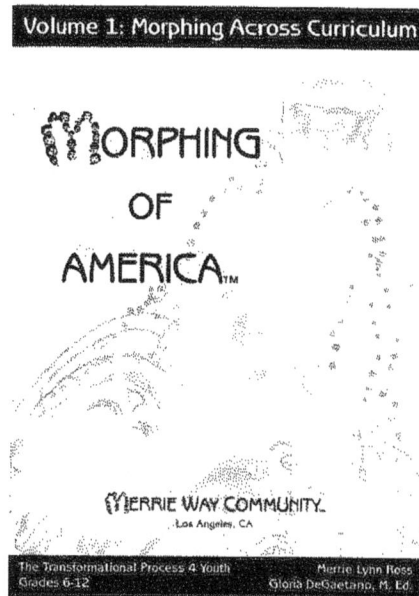

Volume 1: Morphing Across Curriculum

MORPHING

OF

AMERICA™

MERRIE WAY COMMUNITY.
Los Angeles, CA

The Transformational Process 4 Youth   Merrie Lynn Ross
Grades 6-12   Gloria DeGaetano, M. Ed.

Merrie Lynn Ross

Gloria Degaetano m.Ed

In Loving Memory of
my beloved son, Byron Fox

You shine on as a Loving Peacemaker. As our National Spokesperson, you served with exalted enthusiasm, joy and dedication. You're a magical inspiration...touched many hearts in your glorious 22 years.

Your enlivened spirit radiates... your wish for us to...

"BE Real, Laugh & Love"

ACKNOWLEDGMENTS

Heartfelt Gratitude to the amazing global participants in "Morph America." To the students, parents, teachers, administrators for contributing their ingenuity and commitment to bring creative learning and ethics into the classroom. To MerrieWay Community for offering the stellar "Morph America" program and exercises included here. Carol Connors for her inspirational "Morph America" song, lyrics and music. Steve Rotblatt for his awesome cover art design.

We thank our sponsors: Microsoft, Ellis Foundation, Lorsch Family Foundation, Lear Foundation, Roger Dauer, Sheriff Baca, Los Angeles, New York, Texas, and Washington School Districts, Chicago Police Veterans, Darby Mcfarland, Madeline Guzzman, Write Brothers. Philanthropists, community activists, and other contributors, too many to mention, you know who you are.

Your commitment, resourcefulness, and courage sets an example, raises the bar, bringing together the heart and soul of our society... to live the highest ethical standards for the benefit of all.

Bravo to our "Morph America" Youth Anchor team, our masterful mentors, volunteers, and facilitators, who are our Heart Song, spreading unity's light, passing the torch of peace, One by One.

ACKNOWLEDGMENTS OF GRATITUDE

Morphing of America Youth Anchor/National Spokesperson
Byron Fox

Film Mentors
Bob Mendelshon, Ed Mailhot, Derek Grover, Marci & Scott Madden, Irv Kershner, Paul Michael Glazer, Glen Willey, Chuck Norris, Esai Morales, Lee Grant, Michael York, Syd Field, Phylcia Rashad, Michael Nolan, Kathleen Tyner, Paul Bloch, Joe Sohm

Educators
Wendy Becker, Leah Bailey, Alice Britt, Mary Lee Calmes, James Gleason, Dorrie Kurwin, Kevin O'Malley, Lucas Richman, Sheila Lewis, Joe Cash, Paul Cummins, Erica Hagen, Dr. Ilene Kassorla, John Leichey, Nancy Garfield

We want to thank the dedicated administrators, teachers, and facilitators, you know who you are. As participants in Morphing of America, your generosity of spirit and commitment empowered our youth.

Community Mentors
Lyn Davis Lear, Phil Lane, Bob Lorsch, Sheldon Lewis, Dr. Bruce & Susan Harshman, Richard & Daphne Ziman, Peter Bloch, Ilene Proctor, Bobbie Stern, Joanne Fierstein.

May we express our appreciation for the tireless work on behalf of the Morphing of America volunteers, whose radiant examples continue to make Morphing of America a stellar process.

Special Thanks
To Darby MacFarland for her ingenuity and creative spirit.

To Julie Laux for her vital support and her devotion and commitment as a parent.

To Carol Conners, our song bird, for the music and lyrics of the Morphing of America Theme Song.

To Bill, Jan & Aimee Lou Ross for always being there with loving support.

Sponsors
Ellis Foundation
IBM/Aptiva
Adobe
Microsoft
Chromatics

We want to thank the many contributors and friends of Morphing of America for their continuing support enhancing our youth's creative spirit and well being.

Table of Contents

MORPHING IN THE CONTENT AREAS   95

EVALUATION FORMS   139

ORDER FORM   143

Welcome To
MORPHING OF AMERICA™

"The world we have made as a result of the level of thinking we have done thus far creates problems we cannot solve at the same level at which we created them."

—————————————— Albert Einstein ——————————————

Remember this puzzle?

Connect all nine dots using only four lines, **never letting your pencil leave the paper:**

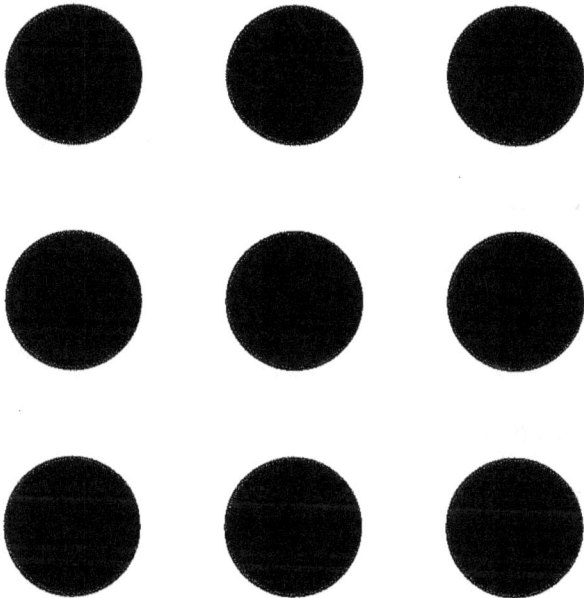

You might recall that this cannot be solved by drawing lines which stay within the confines of the dots. If you box yourself in, there's no way to succeed. The lines drawn must go *beyond* the dots, outside of the imaginary box most of us automatically create. The puzzle is only solved by transcending perceived boundaries.

Morphing of America gives youth a positive voice through opportunities to think in creative ways and to discover innovative approaches to problem solving— to help them "go outside the box" in relationship to themselves and their world. We know that children learn best when they are solving problems that are important to them. With the **Morphing Process**, students choose the topic they want to "morph" and become actively engaged in creating their unique solution. By examining challenging issues in–depth, students gain critical and creative thinking skills, insight into themselves, and affiliation and interrelatedness to peers, family, and community. Students of all ability levels enhance their learning capacity and further their emotional and social development. Participating in a **Morphing Project** means that students are learning by processing their experiences. They become empowered with the thrill of making positive contributions, while improving their intrinsic motivation, self–respect, and self–esteem.

In effect, **Morphing of America** in the classroom takes students to that next level of thinking Einstein considered critical for any long–lasting cultural change. It can move them to perceive the challenges that define our times—changes in the family, our newly global world, the environment, the workplace, the role of technology— with whole new ways of understanding. It will spur students to address the problems of the 21st Century with responsibility, imagination, and wisdom.

As participants in

MORPHING OF AMERICA™

You join others around the nation morphing for a better future.

Participate in national projects with other schools. Create a visual art project, a play, a community service effort, a unique essay, poem or story, an organized event, an invention, a model city, an environmental morph, etc. Remember that all your projects must express a positive point of view. You can photograph your project and send it in for evaluation.

We will recognize student and school achievements. A team of evaluators will be looking at the morphing projects. Special acknowledgement of your work could appear in our newsletter, book, on our website, or even on national TV, or in a special film!

You have the opportunity to participate in the Annual Morphing of America Film and Video Festival Send in a copy of your film or video production and be part of this special day!

Visit our website and link with other Morphing of America Schools and create potential collaborations. www.morphamerica.org

Send morphing projects or photos of the projects to our national headquarters:

MORPHING OF AMERICA™

13601 Ventura Bvd., Suite 227

Sherman Oaks, CA 91423

Goals of the National Morphing of America Project

Morphing Projects allow teachers to use a hands–on approach to learning which can easily be integrated into any curricular area. Specifically a **Morphing Project** will:

* combine left and right brain teaching activities, using powerful educational strategies to meet the needs of all learning styles.

* bridge the arts and technology by offering projects which allow students to use video and computer, along with artistic input such as drawing, dancing, drama, music, etc.

* teach students a process for problem solving which they can apply to any given situation for the rest of their lives.

* enhance students' ability to cope with stress and complex problems which can seem overwhelming by empowering them to know how to use their higher level thinking skills and creativity to effect positive change.

* promote cooperative learning and team building, emphasizing cooperation rather than individual competition and teaching students important aspects of group dynamics and the value of working with others toward a common goal.

* provide opportunities for community service, showing how to effect change on grassroots levels and allowing students experiences to feel needed and to make a difference.

* encourage cultural literacy by providing a global approach to learning and by emphasizing the value of diversity when meeting life's challenges.

* motivate students to take dynamic action and use their innate talents to contribute to their world.

* give students important decision–making skills, promoting responsibility to self, family, peers, school, and community.

* enhance student's competence and confidence as they explore, create, and express themselves in matters that are meaningful to them.

10

Bravo!
You're on the
Morphing of America Team

"Morphing issues you care about... is history in the making."

Morphing of America was initiated by veteran filmmakers... like myself. Educators, parents, youth, corporate sponsors, and the community at large have helped create this awesome opportunity for you... America's youth.

Your contributions are the most valuable and vital part of this program.
Your voice will be heard. Your solutions and Morphing projects will be profiled nationally. Your visions expressed in community service, art, film, performing arts, etc. are your unique contributions, offering a positive example and inspiration for youth across the nation.

What to expect from the morphing process:

* You will look inside yourself with courage to explore disturbing issues.

* You and your classmates, as "Morphing Teams," will cooperatively explore the effects of your life choices... on yourself and society.

* You and your classmates will discover the creative space within, where dreams and brilliant ideas are born.

* Research and beneficial soul–searching will help you to achieve understanding, growth, and self–confidence.

* Solutions you discover will become the building blocks for your life path of values and aspirations, knowing there is always more than one hopefull solution to a problem.

Our 'Morph Tools' will help you master optimism, amidst life's challenges. Your self–esteem will flourish as you discover your place as a responsible citizen in the community.

Once you've Learned to Morph you can build upon it. It is a tool to help pave your life journey with courage and originality. Morphing can be taught to family and friends.

"Let's Morph It," is a favorite saying of those students, educators, parents, and mentors who have done it. I am one of those fortunate participants. My perceptions, aspirations and goals have changed. It is an honor and a privilege to Morph our future with committed and inspired youth in America. It is your wholehearted participation in the Morphing Process that will help shape your character, values, and dreams for a positive and enlightened future.

In Gratitude,

Merrie Lynn Ross

Words and Music by
Carol Connors
(ASCAP)

Theme Song for
THE MORPHING OF AMERICA

Moderately

To be all that you can be, face re - a - li - ty and change... change... To see all the dreams you've dreamed come a - live be - fore your eyes, change You can change the world. You can change your - self. It's the MORPH - ING OF A - ME - RI - CA. It's the joy of chang - ing one - self. When no - one's left be - hind and ev - 'ry - bod - y comes a - long, we'll

©1997

C G Am Am7
change... change... When what went wrong be-fore is now
D/A Gadd2
right for ev - er - more, we've changed. It's the
C/G Gadd2 Dm/F
MORPH - ING OF A - ME - RI-CA, the chang - ing of the
C/E Cm/E♭ Gadd2/D C/D
guard. THE MORPH - ING OF A - ME - RI - CA, the
Am7/D D7sus D7 B♭/F
joy in who you are. To be part of life in the
Gadd2 B♭/F Gadd2
pres - ent you must un - mask your face. Take
Amadd2 Am7 D
cour-age in be - ing the first, not the last in chang-ing the hu - man
D7 C Gadd2
race. See the tears of dis - ap - point - ment dis - ap -
C/G Gadd2 C/G
pear be - fore your eyes. It's the dawn - ing of A -

Gadd2 Am7 D7sus D7 E♭7sus E♭7
me-ri-ca, the joy of be-ing a-live... a-live! It's the
D♭/A♭ A♭add2 D♭/A♭
MORPH-ING OF A-ME-RI-CA. It's the chang-ing of the
A♭add2 D♭/A♭ A♭add2
guard. It's the MORPH-ING OF A-ME-RI-CA, the
B♭m7 E♭7sus E♭7 E7sus E7
joy in who you are! It's the
D/A Aadd2 D/A
MORPH-ING OF A-ME-RI-CA. It's the chang-ing of the
Aadd2 D/A Aadd2
guard. It's the MORPH-ING OF A-ME-RI-CA, the
Bm7 E13 D
joy in who you are!
Dm6 Aadd2

Chapter 1

Morphing:
A Transformational Process

Teaching problem-solving can be a very frustrating experience. First, of all when dealing with a problem requiring a sequence of thought, students very often give up. They find the experience of slowly working through a problem too slow, time-consuming, and mentally challenging to be a satisfying experience. Secondly, students usually "get it" at the level they are working and cannot see beyond the immediate task. Learning to solve a math problem, for instance, they do not know how to take what they learned in math class and apply the basic elements of problem solving to other areas in their lives. Working out math problems is not related to solving personal problems in the traditional ways we experience teaching and learning. Transference of learning is not taking place because transference of problem solving skills is dependent upon intentional teaching of problem-solving methods, approaches, and attitudes. Morphing of America gives the previously missing "hook" that arouses students' curiosity and reactivates their zest for learning. In the same way that Einstein tapped creativity and the imagination and used it as a powerful thinking tool, we want to we want to bring that spirit of learning back into the schools.

Let's face it, in today's schools, the thinking skill crisis continues to grow, along with the number of teens who are frustrated, alienated, and out of touch with their innate problem-solving abilities. A new paradigm for teaching students to address and solve problems is in order. This morphing manual proposes a new paradigm for conceiving how to teach students problem solving and delivers research based, classroom-tested, practical ways to engage students best thinking and originality.

Student inquiry is the focus throughout a morphing project. Like many teachers, you are probably familiar with the term, inquiry. Over the past few years inquiry has received much attention and is considered innovative and cutting edge methodology. In reality inquiry is not new, Socrates knew the importance of "learning through questioning" and countless teachers since have understood the tremendous benefits of helping children develop inquiring minds by allowing them to explore their curiosities.

The morphing process integrates three basic areas to help students use inquiry effectively:

* Personal meaning and subjective experiences

* Concrete knowledge from books and others' experiences

* Symbolic expressions such as art, music, dance, drama

This process is unique.

The following characteristics distinguish it from traditional problem–solving processes, making it so necessary and valuable in today's classroom:

* The **Morphing Solution–Finding Process** is a transformational one. It is not only linear but activates both subconscious and conscious thinking; enabling the student to use high levels of thought and deep wells of creativity.

* In the **Morphing Process** the *process of arriving at the solution* is as critical as the solution. In fact, more so, because it is the *process* which empowers the student to learn to generate an endless supply of solutions. It is learning the *process* which makes for effective transference to unlimited life experiences.

* In the **Morphing Process** there is not One Solution. Solutions are temporary, not static, taking many shapes and forms. By emphasizing fluidity, context, and dynamic growth, students come to realize that a great variety of solutions could be "right." In this process, the morphed problem or situation is actually a changed reality.

* The **Morphing Process** assumes students will use personal knowing in addition to book knowledge. And since student inquiry is at the heart of a morphing project, using personal knowing is a requirement!

* The **Morphing Process** moves from the student to encompass larger spheres of influence. The student is always the center.

As students participate in the **Morphing Process**, every positive action leads to a gradual change in attitudes and values. That, in turn, changes the expectations of what they are capable of doing. The more they morph, then, the more students will see themselves as creative, ever–growing individuals whose wisdom and clarity continually reach out to larger and larger spheres of influence.

Once learned, the Morphing Process changes everything— how students define problems; how possibilities are conceived; how solutions are approached; and most importantly, *how students perceive themselves.*

While participating in a **Morphing Project**, self–concept soars. Students learn that they *can* effect positive change. Students have many opportunities to experience their minds as splendid tools, magnificently designed for unlimited potential. Students come to know and respect their internal power to create. And it is this knowing that is so transformational...

The transformational problem–solving process outlined below, provides students with the skeleton for any morphing process— whether producing a video, writing an essay, or making a collage. Through it they will experience a myriad of ways to direct conscious thought for creative purposes and morph, not only solutions, but their own thinking processes as well. Please be clear that you don't have to use all the steps given. Have fun and let the current of your students' enthusiasm direct the problem–solving sequence. After some familiarity with the process, your students will probably adapt it or make up variations that take them on even higher levels of thinking! Encourage this type of innovation each step along the way as soon as you and your students feel comfortable doing so.

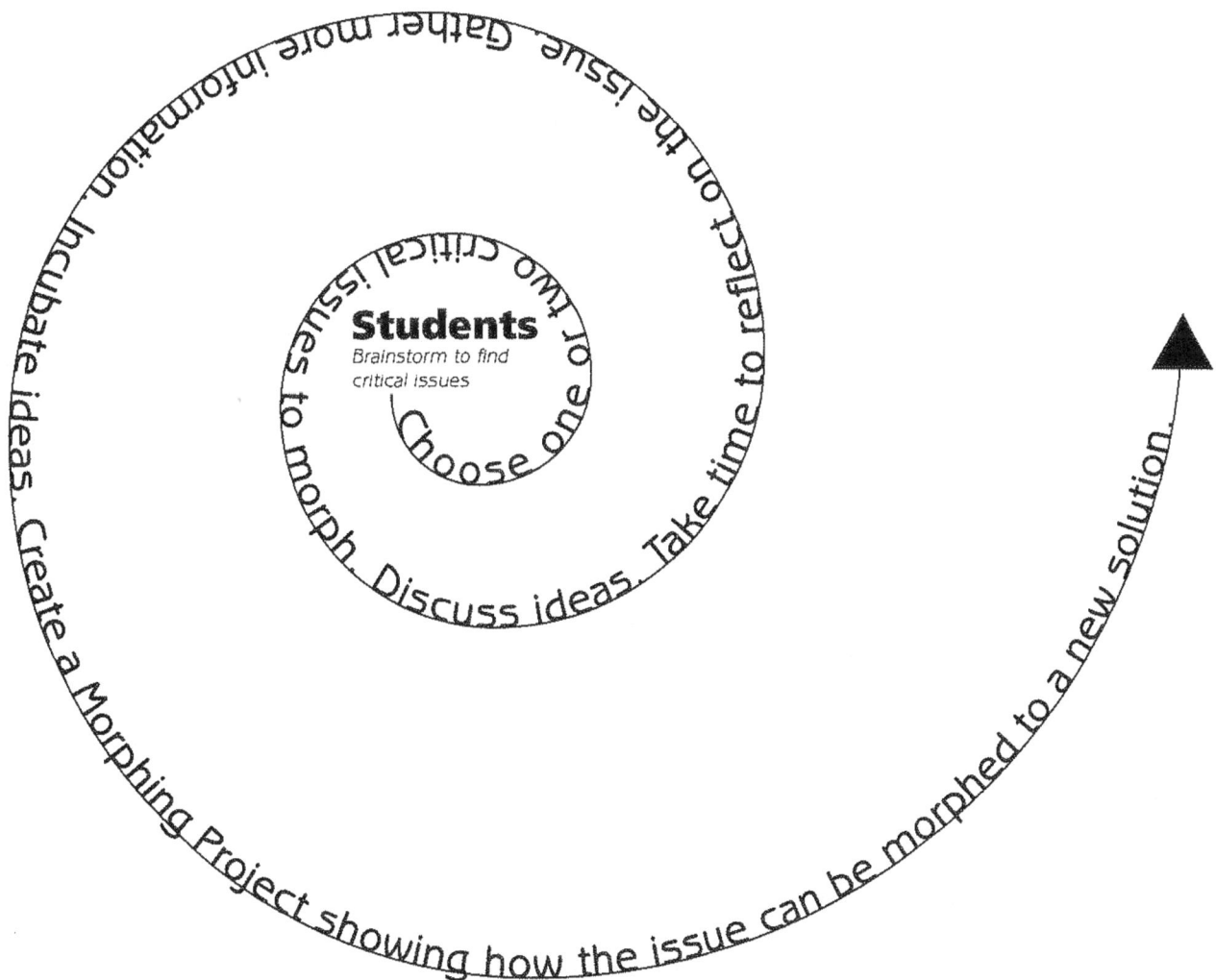

Spiral diagram (read from center outward): **Students** Brainstorm to find critical issues. Choose one or two critical issues to morph. Discuss ideas. Take time to reflect on the issue. Gather more information. Incubate ideas. Create a Morphing Project showing how the issue can be morphed to a new solution.

Transformational
Problem–Solving

While participating in a **Morphing of America Project**, students are asked to address, perceive, and decipher critical issues that are important to them keeping the following definition in mind:

morphing — to superimpose one image, thought, concept over another; to improve; to transform; to find positive solutions to human issues and concerns; to evolve and create a vision of hope and inspiration for humanity, building the bridge into the coming millennium.

STEP 1

Students brainstorm ideas to find a situation that needs to be morphed—something that they feel very passionate about.

The issue can be as complex as "the homeless in America" or as personal as "getting myself to floss more often." What matters the most here is that the identified problem matters to the student. If you are using this process within a certain curricula area to teach specific content, make sure that you give students a range of problem choices. For instance, if your aim is to teach about the environmental crisis, students could pick from a list of topics such as: the depletion of the ozone layer, the destruction of the rainforests, toxins in water supplies, or the impact of North American's consumer habits on the environment. While brainstorming consider the following:

* Explain that speed is important here. You are trying to get as many ideas on the list as possible. You may want to put a time limit to the session, to encourage the students to think fast.

* Explain that there are no judgments to be made, no comments stated about anyone's ideas. Nothing is limited. Everything is possible. Very often students will grunt or moan when someone says something that seems off–the–wall. Explain that such remarks are unacceptable and that off–the–wall ideas often lead to brilliant ones. Reinforce as much as possible that you want innovative responses and responses that might seem "weird." The students should focus on coming up with ideas and not on responding to what others are saying. It's extremely important that students know their imaginations have free reign during this process and that they are safe to risk–take. Encourage students to encourage each other.

* The facilitator of the session should refrain from making any remarks, especially from praising any ideas. The only thing to say is, "What else...?"

* After the outpouring, keep the list prominent in the students' range of vision— either displayed in the classroom or on papers in individual notebooks. Tell the students that no judgments or evaluations are to be made at this point as to which problems are really important here and which are not. This process was to lay out possibilities only. If each student in your class is working with a different issue, have small groups take turns brainstorming for each other. This can be a very powerful group activity because when students have not worked at gathering data about a problem, they may be more likely to come up with fresh ideas.

STEP 2

Students now review their brainstormed topic lists and vote on the two most important issues with the goal to narrow to one issue, the most critical one, if they can.
If students are inspired by more than one issue, that's OK. Instead of the class morphing one issue, four or five issues can be morphed!

STEP 3

Students share their ideas, feelings, opinions, biases, and personal experiences about the issue in an open forum.
The teacher should keep facilitating a variety of questions to get as much sharing as possible. Model active listening for the students and keep asking questions to continue the energy and enthusiasm with the purpose to evolve compelling questions and ideas. Point out to the students that their questions about the issue are as important as anything they think they know about the issue.

STEP 4

Students take time to reflect on the issue.
During this time:

*   Lead students in a relaxation technique and/or reflective time such as turning lights down. Put soft music on in order to emphasize the need for them to get in touch with their inner voices on the issue and all the ideas so far. First they are to focus on the problems surrounding the issue, the impressions, the frustrations, the fears, the pain, the sadness.

*   After several minutes, invite them to write down their impressions and experience.

*   Then the teacher repeats the same relaxation technique asking them to reflect on possible solutions. We ask them to dream the unspeakable dream—the place of hope, of vision—to go into that space where creativity flourishes.

*   **Encourage them that anything is possible here.** This is the place of wonderment—of their creative solutions. After a few minutes ask the students to open their eyes, remain very quiet and write down their solutions and then share them with the other students.

STEP 5

Students gather more information on the issue.
Using a variety of sources, students find out as much about the issue as possible. Sources could be:

*   personal knowledge and experience, including writing reflections in personal journal entries and interviewing others;

*   knowledge systems, including the library, the Internet, books, magazines, and newspapers;

*   communication systems such as: art, role play or improvisation in order deepen their understanding and relationship to the issue. Encouraging students to use symbolic communication forms in creative ways can activate their imaginations and help them access information in surprisingly accurate and wonderful ways!

Bring back the information they found out, share it with the class, and discuss it. Through sharing, they can start taking a look at what type of project their collective opinions might best fit. Encourage students to start thinking about what type of project will best express their morphed issue.

STEP 6

Students incubate ideas.
During this stage, nothing is directly being done to further the process. Explain to your students that the subconscious needs time to mull over all the data so far accumulated. Instruct the students that it's very important they not think consciously about their problem or the upcoming project. Their subconscious will work on it better if they give their minds a rest. Whenever they find themselves thinking about it, have them give their minds a nudge and instruct it to think of something else. This may seem strange at first to some students, but the more they learn to honor this incubation stage of the problem–solving process, the more they will invent a truly creative, innovative morphed solution.

STEP 7

From the composite of their shared ideas, students agree and create their morphing project showing how the provocative issue can be morphed to a new solution, their vision for a better future.
The students work alone, in small groups, or as a class and create a project which they eventually share with others to show their morphed solution.

Afterwards...
Take time for students to reflect on the process. Discuss with your students what they gained from this process and how they, themselves, have been morphed! You and the students can fill out the evaluation forms found in the back of this manual and send them into our national headquarters.

7 Easy Steps to MORPHING

1
Brainstorm ideas to find a situation to be morphed.

2
Review the brainstormed list and select one issue, if possible.

3
Hold an open forum of discussion on the issue.

4
Take time to reflect on the issue.

5
Gather more information.

6
Incubate ideas.

7
Agree on a morphing project!

The following pages contain

ten morph tools

which you can use with *any topic* to be morphed.

They are tools specifically designed to help students

deepen the

problem-solving process.

24

CHOOSING AN ISSUE TO MORPH

What do you care about that needs changing?

That's the key question when trying to decide on an issue to morph. Take a moment and think about some possibilities:

_____ Personal issues such as: _____

time   **family**   **friends**

stress   **school**

health

_____ General issues such as: _____

drugs   **the environment**   **gangs**

violence   **poverty**

racism

_____ Other issues that you can think of: _____

_____

_____

Now select three issues from the above lists that seem interesting to you:

_____

_____

_____

If you answer the following questions for each of the three issues you selected on a separate sheet of paper or if you discuss the answers with a parent or friend, chances are you have some good ideas on where to begin!

1.   How much do I care about this issue?

2.   Am I motivated to find out more information about it? Why?

3.   Does addressing the issue seem exciting to me in some way?

4.   How can working on a project related to this issue affect me? How can it affect others?

5.   If I choose this issue, will I feel like I have done something worth my time and energy?

Morph Tool #2

BE AN INFORMATION DETECTIVE

When you morph something, having information from a variety of sources can help you see your issues in different ways, from different viewpoints. The more information you have, the better the chances are that you will come up with an outrageous, spectacular morph. To gather information you can: think by yourself, talk with people, read, go to the library, watch television, and make observations. Think of yourself as a detective who is on the path of important clues. On the lines below list the people you will talk to and the places you could go to get information about your topic:

_____

_____

_____

_____

_____

_____

_____

_____

_____

_____

Now decide what you will do first, second, third, etc. and write your steps in the spaces below. You may only have one or two steps and that's OK. If it will help you, talk to a friend or parent for ideas.

My Action Plan for Gathering Information

1._____

2._____

3._____

4._____

Below are potential sources of information you could use during your morphing project. Put a check beside the ones you are most likely to use.

Information from Yourself, Friends, and Community

____ something you experienced first hand

____ information a friend passed on to you

____ a story a grandparent told you

____ an experience a friend or relative had while on vacation

____ something you "just know" through common knowledge or your intuition

____ facts you remember being told when you were younger

____ common beliefs held by your parents

____ something you learned at a school assembly

____ e-mail messages from pen pals

____ a thought which pops into your head while you are taking a walk

____ information you could get by interviewing people at school or in your community

Information from Books and Other Content Sources

____ the library

____ the Internet

____ school textbooks

____ encyclopedias and dictionaries

____ magazines

____ newspapers

____ professional journals

____ TV or video guides

____ TV programs, videos, video and computer games

Information from Sign/Symbol Sources

____ an idea you got while doing an art project

____ something that came to you while journaling

____ information you can get by role-playing the situation

____ ideas that occur to you while listening to music or playing an instrument

____ ideas you could get from reading a poem

____ thoughts that come while dancing the issue

____ information that comes to you while communicating with others

LOOK AGAIN!

OK. You have considered an issue, got information on it, thought a lot about it. Now's the time to take a step back and look at it again. After all that work has your issue changed considerably? Are you dealing with a different issue from when you started this process? Do you want to change your issue a bit because of the information you gathered?

The questions below can help you sort out your thoughts.
Read through them and discuss them with a friend or in class or answer them on a separate sheet of paper.

1. Does your issue seem bigger than when you started? In what way?

2. Does your issue seem smaller than when you started? In what way?

3. How have your ideas changed so far?

4. What are the three most important things you learned about your issue during the information–gathering stage?

5. Have your feelings about the issue changed? If, so in what way?

6. Did opinions from friends affect how you feel about your issue?

7. What advice have others given you during this process?

8. What advice have you given yourself during this process?

9. Is there something new about the issue you researched that is interesting to you? If so, what?

10 If you could change your issue to be morphed in any way, what would you do?

After you have considered these questions use the space below to redefine your direction:
The problem, situation, or issue I will morph has changed to become:

_____

_____

_____

_____

_____

GUIDELINES FOR INDIVIDUAL BRAINSTORMING

The purpose of brainstorming is to get as many ideas down on paper as possible. It is not a time for judging or evaluating the worth of the ideas. Rather, it is a time to encourage your imagination to flow free and easy. When you are brainstorming by yourself, follow the steps below for maximum effect!

Step One: Get comfortable. Relax and take some deep breaths.
Have plenty of paper available and a pen or pencil.
Set a timer for five minutes.

Step Two: Say to yourself, "I am going to write down all the ideas I can think of about ___. I will not censor any idea. I will not judge any idea. I will encourage myself to keep thinking when I feel like I can't think of anything else."

Step Three: Begin writing down your ideas. But watch that little voice inside you that is saying this is a good idea or that's a rotten idea, or that's weird—try not to pay too much attention to that voice. Counter with another voice that keeps asking, "What else can I think of?"

Step Four: When the timer goes off, set it again and write for another five minutes.

Step Five: When you are finished, read over your list. Can you think of anything else to add? Go ahead and do that.

Step Six: Read your list again and circle all the ideas you think are interesting and creative.

From this brainstorming session with myself I discovered:

_____

_____

_____

_____

_____

_____

_____

_____

_____

_____

Morph Tool #6

GUIDELINES FOR GROUP BRAINSTORMING

The purpose of brainstorming is to get as many ideas down on paper as possible. It is not a time for judging or evaluating the worth of the ideas. Rather, it is a time to encourage your imagination to flow free and easy. When you are brainstorming with a group, follow the steps below for maximum effect!

Step One: Choose a group leader. The leader will record the brainstorming ideas on a large piece of butcher paper or on a whiteboard or blackboard.

Step Two: The leader reminds the group. "Our purpose is to get as many ideas down as possible in a short amount of time (five or ten minutes). No talking or discussing the ideas. No judging. No comments." After noting the time or setting a timer, the leader tells the group to begin.

Step Three: The members of the group calls out ideas while the leader records them.

Step Four: When ideas are coming slowly the leader keeps asking, "What else can you think of?"

Step Five: When everyone is finished giving ideas, read over the list. Can anyone think of anything else?

Step Six: Read over the list and discuss the ideas now, if you choose to do that as a group. You could also discuss which ideas you like best and why. Circle those ideas you consider the most interesting and creative.

What I learned about myself from participating in a group brainstorming session:

_____

_____

_____

_____

PICTURE POSSIBILITIES

Possibility thinking means thinking "What if?" Answer the questions below to think about far–out possibilities.

What if the issue, problem, or situation you morphed

could talk? What would it say?

could walk? Where would it go?

could sing? Who would listen?

could express feelings? How does it feel?

could solve itself? What does it think about your ideas?

See if you can come up with your own "What If?" questions. Then use the space below to sketch different possible solutions for your issue. What are some ways it could look like once it is morphed? Does asking "What if?" questions help you see more possible solutions? Why or why not?

Morph Tool #8

NO LIMIT!

Your brain has unlimited potential. In fact, the human brain has been called "the three–pound universe" because of its vast potential.

Using the brain helps to develop it. In that way the brain is like a muscle, when you use it, it grows and gets stronger. Thinking will actually grow brain structures called dendrites.

On the dendrites branching out from the brain cell below, write in those activities which provide you with mental challenges. They can be activities that you already enjoy doing or activities you want to try. Can you put a thinking activity on each dendrite? If you can, you are well on your way to developing your full brain capacity...

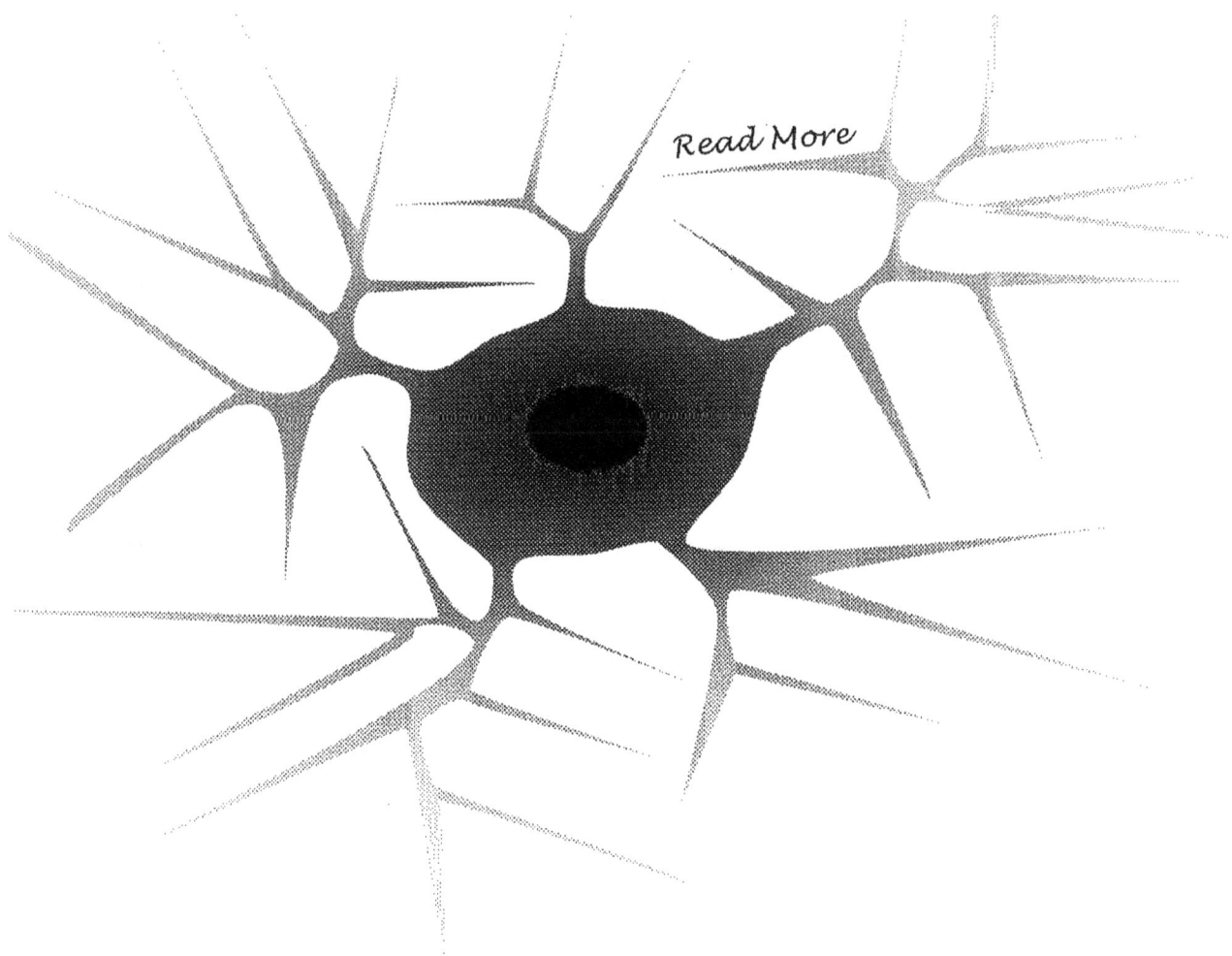

Read More

Morph Tool # 9

SOLUTION FINDING

In the spaces provided list the associated problems and possible solutions of the issue you have been working with. You may copy them from your brainstormed lists.

Associated Problems

Possible Solutions

_____   _____

_____   _____

_____   _____

_____   _____

_____   _____

_____   _____

Now explain to a partner what is most important from both lists. Respond to clarifying questions from your partner and describe what is most important to you as completely as possible.

In the space below with the help of your partner, write solutions or changes you want to make regarding this issue, problem, or situation.

_____

_____

_____

_____

_____

_____

_____

When you are finished, listen to your partner explain what is important about his/her issue, ask clarifying questions, and help your partner come up with a variety of solutions.

Morph Tool # 10

DISSOLVE AND SUPERIMPOSE

Have a friend or a teacher read the following to you while you relax with your eyes closed:

Imagine the problem situation you have identified. See it as clearly as you can. See it in vivid colors. Hear any sounds associated with it. *(At this point wait a few minutes, then say):*

Shake your head, yes, if you have a clear picture in your mind. *(Wait until you get a "yes" before going on.)*

Now, alongside of a picture of your problem, see one of the solutions you put on your brainstorming list. See the image of this solution as vividly as possible with lots of color. Feel the positive feelings inside of you that come when you think of this solution.

Do you see this image right beside the other image? *(Wait for a yes, before going on.)*

As you hold the two images together, see the solution, the image you want to create, start to move and become bigger. See the problem shrinking and dissolving. Keep dissolving the problem. Now put the solution on top of the problem. Do this until the problem is completely dissolved and the solution has taken its place.

Now the image of the solution is filling your entire mind. Relax and be with the solution for a while. *(Stop talking for a few minutes. Then say:)*

What is happening now? Who is there? How does this solution make you feel? See the important things in the solution that you should remember.

When you feel like it, open your eyes and in the space below, write what you want to remember about the superimposed image in your mind:

_____

_____

_____

_____

_____

_____

Chapter 2

Applying the

MORPHING PROCESS

Tools for Conducting a Morphing of America Project

Think of this manual as a toolbox for you, the teacher, to pick and choose what is most appropriate for your students. The topics and activities have been designed intentionally for adapting to the wide variety of student needs found in today's classroom. Therefore, you have everything you need to conduct a highly successful **Morphing of America Project**, no matter what your classroom resources might be. Below is an outline of the essential components you will want to use with your students throughout a typical morphing project:

The Morphing Process

As described in Chapter 1, this step–by–step outline shows you the basic sequence of the morphing process. Of course, you won't always use all seven steps nor would you want to! Also, your sequence may vary depending on the time you have to conduct a morphing project. You may want to duplicate the steps of this process on page 22, laminate it, and keep it on your desk for easy reference. Also, give students a copy of it so they will know what to anticipate as they move through the process.

Teacher Prep Sheets:

These sheets give you an overview of the topic to be morphed and suggested questions to ask students throughout the process.

Student Morph Tools:

These activities can be used at various times throughout the process to help students examine the issue more thoroughly, to gather additional information, and to practice team–building and group interaction skills. Many of the activities can be expanded into a more involved morphing project, if you wish.

Morphing Projects:

Brief descriptions of possible projects are included so the students will have some idea of the scope of the types of activities they can do for a **Morphing of America Project**. These are purposefully written to the student in language they can understand, so that the teacher may duplicate them and pass them out for the students to discuss and choose. You may find that some of the projects will require little time on your part, while others are general ideas which will need you to fill in the specifics. By all means, guide the students in their choice. *But it is extremely important that the students decide what project to do.* It's OK if they do not choose any of the projects listed. As a matter of fact, that's to be expected. In many instances, students will come up with a unique project they are excited about or you may want to guide students to think seriously about a project you would like to see them do. The bottom line, however, is that the students feel ownership about their morphing project.

The **Morphing Process** can be as complex or as simple as you want to make it. Start with the key statement: "Choose a critical issue and morph it to show how it will be in the 21st Century." Then use the tools set out in this manual to take your students where they want to go. If you find yourself getting sidetracked these three guidelines will help bring you back on course:

* **Emphasize divergent over convergent thinking.** One of the basic strengths of the morphing process is that it relies on students' inherent creativity. It is less a problem–solving method and so much more a creative–solution finding process. By keeping questions and activities as open–ended as possible, students will have more opportunities for originality and innovation.

* **Balance analysis with synthesis.** Cutting edge thinkers in the 21st Century will be balanced thinkers, using both left and right hemispheres equally. **Point out** to the students when an activity is more linear and when one is more multi—dimensional. For instance, when doing a paper and pencil thinking process, explain to the students that their left–brains will be working overtime. And when doing a drama performance or an art activity, **explain** the workings of their right brains and how these types of activities are much more open–ended and free-wheeling. **Ask** them to observe which types of activities they like better, which they naturally gravitate to. This morphing process is actually a marriage of sequential and random thinking activities and will give students many opportunities to become adept at both.

* **Have students keep a journal throughout the process.** The heart of the morphing process is helping students discover and mobilize their inner resources. Journaling can be a very effective way to examine and explore those inner resources. It also can serve as an effective metacognitive activity to enable students to become conscious about how the morphing process is affecting them and how they have affected the process. Each day **set aside** 10–15 minutes for students to put on paper what they are thinking, feeling, envisioning. As they work through the morphing project, students continue writing journal entries. **Encourage** reading of past entries and discussion in small groups of the changes they have experienced in themselves and in others during the time they were involved in morphing. Some of the morph tools suggest students write in their journals for a specific purpose. Students can **compare** these entries with their stream–of–consciousness entries to learn which types of assignments evoke their most substantial thinking.

Morphing: Getting Started — An example for you

How do you use the tools in this manual for maximum effectiveness? The best way is to show you. Below you will find an example which takes a fictitious group of 8th grade students through a morphing process, using the seven steps outlined in Chapter 1. Reference is made to the various book's components, so that you have suggestions for when and how best to use them.

Step 1: Brainstorm ideas to find a situation to be morphed.

What do these students feel passionate about? Their responses include:

homelessness	divorce	self–esteem in youth
drugs	gun control	teen pregnancy
racism	unkind people	stress
future job opportunities	homework	date rape

Step 2: Review the brainstormed list and select one issue, if possible.

These students broke into small groups to discuss the issues and to decide which one they would want to morph. It turned out that the class agreed *self esteem in youth* would be an interesting topic to morph.

Step 3: An open forum of discussion on youth self–esteem is held.

During this time, students shared ideas, feelings, personal experiences. These discussions could last one class session or longer. The point is to stir up the waters and give students many ideas to think about. *During this session the teacher can use:*

*   the questions on the Teacher Prep Sheet to spur discussion

*   one or two of the Student Morph Tools to add topics for discussion

Step 4: Students take time to reflect on the issue.

The teacher took students through a visualization technique in which the students remembered a time when their self–esteem was at a low point. They were encouraged to see this situation as vividly in their mind's eye as possible. Then they wrote their impressions of this situation. Next, they visualized a time when they felt very confident and secure with good self–esteem. They were to feel each moment of this experience as deeply as possible. Then afterwards, they wrote down their impressions of this experience, with encouragement from the teacher to also list the ways poor self esteem could be morphed into a solid sense of self–esteem. The students spent quiet time then reflecting on this.

Step 5: Gather more information.

As part of the morphing process, the teacher wanted the students to learn more about what goes into a person with self-esteem. So she had them research Maslow's hierarchy of self-actualization. The students compared his ideas with their qualities that they listed in the step above. The teacher also used Morph Tools # 2 and 3 to further discuss what effects a person's self-esteem and how to morph disappointments and keep a grounded self-esteem in tact. *At this point any of the Morph Tools may be used for topic exploration.*

Step 6: Students incubate ideas.

Students took a day off from thinking about the process to incubate ideas and see if anything else would emerge.

Step 7: Students agree on a morphing project.

The teacher duplicated and passed out the sheet, Morphing Projects, self-esteem. As a class they discussed each one. They also discussed any new ideas that came out of their incubation period. The teacher asked the question: "What type of project will best show our creative solutions for morphing self esteem?"

After discussion, two ideas emerged. One group wanted to create confidence boosters for the school as outlined in suggestion 4. They thought that it would help kids at the school if they were daily reminded of how great they were. They also thought it would help school morale. The other half of the class wanted to break into teams to produce a Public Service Announcement and air it on a local TV station which they knew had made a commitment to help youth. Because the teacher was familiar with the video production process, she agreed with this project.

You can use the following pages,

if *your* students decide to do

a morph on self–esteem. This is the format

you will find throughout the manual.

Enjoy the morphing process…

Teacher Prep Sheet
Self-Esteem

Changing any negative view of ourselves may take time since self-concept is imbedded in our core emotional response systems. In other words, how we feel about ourselves is not usually logical. Rather it is the sum of how we emotionally responded to the conscious and unconscious messages of our early caregivers. How were these messages about self received? distorted? interpreted?

In this section, students will have the opportunity to examine the issue of self-esteem, as in-depth as you want to take them. Below are questions which will help you facilitate this journey:

1.   In your own words, define self-esteem.

2.   What are important components of self-esteem?

3.   Describe someone with a healthy self-esteem; someone with poor self-esteem.

4.   What do you do to feel good about yourself?

5.   How does blaming others affect your self-esteem?

6.   Would you have a better self-esteem if you were born to different parents, lived in different times, went to a different school? Why or why not?

7.   Who do you admire? What is their self-esteem like?

8.   How does making goals and plans affect your self-esteem?

9.   What makes you feel bad about yourself?

10.   How do people with a healthy self-esteem solve problems?

11.   How does what you contribute to others affect your self-esteem?

12.   What are you doing when you feel the best about yourself?

13.   When are you most apt to be self-critical?

14.   What do you say to yourself about yourself?

15.   When young children have a poor self-esteem, what might be the consequences later in their lives?

16.   When someone puts you down or calls you a name, how does that affect your self-esteem?

17.   Do rules help or hurt your sense of self-esteem?

18.   How do you show yourself you appreciate yourself?

19.   How do your decisions affect your self-esteem?

20.   If you could do one thing to enhance your self-esteem, what would that be?

DREAMS CAN HELP

How we feel about ourselves has been called, self–esteem, and includes self–respect and self–love. The level of our self–esteem basically determines our level of success in life. Every decision we make, every action we take stems first from how we feel about ourselves and our talents and capabilities.

Feeling good about ourselves can be considered an art. It takes practice, perseverance during troubling times, and gentle daily reminders of our uniqueness and specialness.

What are your hopes and dreams? Below list your hopes and dreams and beside each write the inner personality traits which can assist you in achieving those dreams:

Hopes and Dreams   **Personality Traits Which Can Help Me**

_____   _____

_____   _____

_____   _____

_____   _____

_____   _____

_____   _____

_____   _____

_____   _____

_____   _____

_____   _____

WHAT AFFECTS YOUR SELF-ESTEEM?

How do your feelings of self-esteem and self-worth presently include those needed traits to reach your goals? Which traits would you like to increase in your personality? How can you do this?

Different people react differently to the same situation. For example, a friend you know may feel totally devastated and ugly and bad about herself if she doesn't get invited to the prom. Another friend takes the situation in stride. Shrugs it off and goes on with her life. Does this person have a higher level of self-esteem than the one who feels bad?

With a partner discuss what affects your level of self-esteem. Take turns sharing information. See if you can figure out what will most likely trigger self-criticism, negative self-talk, or low levels of self esteem. Below are some situations you may want to discuss. How do you feel about yourself when encountering them? What do you do to protect your self-esteem? Think of other situations, don't limit yourself to these!

* You have worked so long and so hard, but you don't get picked for the team

* You borrowed a CD from a friend, forgot to get it back on time and your friend has called you, "inconsiderate."

* You flunked an important test.

* You like to read and some "friends" have taken to calling you a "nerd."

* You are an excellent athlete, but some jealous people make fun of you.

* An adult you care about (teacher, parent, etc.) says something derogatory to you.

Some people are more prone to equate a difficult circumstance with how they feel about themselves. We say that they "take things personally." These people are likely to be Feeler personality styles. Thinkers, on the other hand, operate more in an objective world and tend to be more realistic about what happens to them. They can distance themselves more easily from what other people think or say about them. Are you a thinker or a feeler?

MORPHING DISAPPOINTMENTS

In a perfect world we would always get what we want and things would go smoothly. But that is not the way things usually work out. If we are fully engaged in living, disappointments are to be expected. How can we morph a disappointment when it comes our way so it won't get us down about ourselves?

What we say to ourselves about the disappointment is the most important thing. Because guess what? We believe what we tell ourselves! If we tell ourselves we were dumb and stupid for not being invited to the party, then we will feel dumb and stupid. If we keep up this line of thought for every disappointment that comes our way, we can expect to start acting dumb and stupid. How will that then affect our self–esteem?

By practicing positive self–messages when we encounter a disappointment, we will be training our minds to think well of ourselves and be in a much better frame to handle the disappointment so it doesn't hurt our self–esteem.

Here are some things you can say to yourself when you must face a disappointment:

* I have done my best and can't control the outcome. I can feel good about doing my best.

* I won't like being the only one not invited, but I can handle this. I know I am a good person.

* Not every person is going to want to be a good friend. I'll concentrate on the ones who want to be my friend.

* It's tough right now, but I know that I have the strength and courage to come out on top.

Below write out some positive self–messages that you will want to practice. For a length of time, keep track of when and how you use these statements. Are they working for you?

_____

_____

_____

_____

_____

PRAISE YOURSELF

Be your own cheerleader! Valuable research has been done on this. In a book entitled, *Enhancing Self-Esteem* (Frey and Carloch, Accelerated Development, Inc., 1989) the authors explain that a ratio of five praises to every one criticism is needed to counteract the negative.

Most of us find it hard to give ourselves a compliment or tell ourselves how great we are. One way to practice praise is to hold a brag session.

Here is how it works:

Get together with several friends. Sit in a circle. Talk about yourself and say only good things. That's right, brag. Everyone else looks at you and keeps quiet until you are done. Then they ask you, "Anything else?" And you try to keep going with your brag session as long as possible. Then it is someone else's turn to brag.

At first this may feel uncomfortable, so let other people brag about you before you brag about yourself.

Below list all the wonderful things you can say about yourself in an upcoming brag session:

_____

_____

_____

_____

_____

_____

_____

_____

_____

_____

_____

Morphing Projects
Self-Esteem

1 **Produce Public Service Announcements to air on your local TV station.**
Make PSA's about enhancing self-esteem in a world of pressures and stresses. Use what you have learned during the morphing process to give others healthy and hopeful messages about self-esteem.

2 **Create a Positive Message Center.**
Maybe it's a bulletin board, maybe a bowl with cards or slips of paper in it, maybe a nook with motivating reading materials and audio tapes. Create a place in your home, classroom, or school where a person can go to get renewed and receive lots of positive messages for enhancing his/her self esteem.

3 **Establish A Special Recognition Day.**
Organize a schoolwide Recognition Day for showing everyone in some way that they are a valued member of the school community. Hold brag sessions, make up and give out Certificates of Appreciation, do a bunch of good deeds, take time to point out how important everyone is, how much they are needed and how much their own special talents and abilities are appreciated.

4 **Mentor a Younger Child.**
Work with a teacher and find out about a younger student who might be experiencing a time of low self-esteem. Spend special time with the youngster on a regular basis and encourage him/her with what you have learned during the morphing process.

5 **Create Confidence Boosters.**
Does your school begin the day with schoolwide announcements? Why not include a confidence booster or an inspirational quote that will help remind students they are important and valued? Your class could develop or compile one confidence booster for each day of the remaining school year. How can this activity morph your school's self-esteem?

An Invitation to You, the Teacher

"Burn out" is so common for today's educators that it is expected; considered "normal." Most of us do experience it at one time or another because teaching can be overwhelming. To compound the issue, often, teachers do not receive the support, respect, or resources needed to stay on top of the job, let alone flourish in it.

Morphing of America recognizes these deep problems and is not trying to gloss over the complexities involved. But **Morphing** is about moving, taking action; changing reality, and envisioning hope. **Morphing** is about creative solution finding that is self–directed and self–satisfying. *The process and its tremendous potential need not be limited to the students only.*

We invite you to try out the process for your own personal or professional growth before sharing it with your students. Effective educational reform begins in the mind and heart of, you, the individual teacher. You can stay open to the changes that you would intrinsically like to see in your teaching. You can become aware of how your experience of the morphing process affects your students. Are they more open? More receptive of what you are offering them?

With the **Morphing Process** *You* can make transformations *NOW* on your own terms. No need to wait for school administrators to change or for more funding to come through. Positive educational change can take place throughout America, immediately, as teachers face, identify, and morph what might be standing in their way to experiencing a fuller, more alive connection with their students and with themselves.

So let's start morphing...
In the following pages you will find:

> * **Questions for reflection**—to help you identify issues you might like to morph
>
> * **Teacher Morph Tools**—to play around with ideas and share them with colleagues
>
> * **Suggested Projects**—to apply the morphing process in your classroom or school

For the Teacher: **Questions for Reflection...**

1. What do I know about my own teaching process?

2. If I could morph anything about this process, what would it be?

3. What part of teaching do I love, but not have time to do?

4. Why am I teaching?

5. How has my teaching changed over the years? my goals? priorities? motivation? enthusiasm?

6. Why did I go into teaching in the first place? If I made that decision for reasons that don't serve me now, How can I morph that?

7. How do I feel when I get up in the morning? ready to go? or dragging?

8. Has my health declined as a result of teaching? If so, why is this happening? How can I morph that?

9. How do I handle the stress of my job? What do I do on a regular basis to relax?

10. How do my students perceive me?

11. Do I let students evaluate me and my teaching? Why or why not?

12. Do I really need extra classes to yet learn someone's else's' teaching techniques? Or do I need to spend more time alone to get in touch with my inner creative core to develop methods that will work for me?

13. How do I involve parents in my classroom?

14. Have I neglected to train them? give them important work to do? Am I afraid to let go of control?

15. How do I collaborate with my peers? Is this exciting to me? How do I model a team spirit to my students?

16. Do I understand my own learning/teaching style? How do I honor my uniqueness? How do I show I respect myself and my abilities?

17. How has my teaching changed over the years?

18. When I think about my future as a teacher, I think...

19. What am I getting out of teaching?

20. What am I giving in my teaching?

21. What in the bureaucracy is hindering me from doing my highest performance possible?

22. Do I feel that the school policy is supporting me? Why or why not?

23. What are my basic daily attitudes towards teaching?

24. What would I need to do to morph these present attitudes?

25. What do I look forward to each day? What do I dread?

26. How best can I improve my teaching? my relationships with students? my relationships with faculty?

Teacher Morph Tool # 1

MORPHING FOR BALANCE

Is your life balanced? Are you finding (making?) time for yourself? Do you have enough time and the right space for regular doses of reflection? What makes you happiest? Feeling the most confident? Are you able to bring those activities into your life consistently throughout the year (and not just during summer vacation)?

Take some time to fill in the chart below. Share your responses with a few friends. Take action on at least two goals for this school year which will bring your life more balance and less stress.

Things I Love To Do Which Fill Me, Energize Me:

Alone	No Planning	No or Little Money	With Others

Things I Do That Drain My Energy:

Can Do Less Often	Can Delegate	Can Trade	Can Stop

Teacher Morph Tool # 2

LESSENING THE LOAD

How can you make your life at school easier? Below are some areas to look at for possible morphing throughout the year.

Homework: Do I really need to give so much of it?

* How do I know when homework assignments are being effective? What does the research say?

* Can students work in homework teams to correct some of the homework themselves?

* Can I set up peer editing groups for help correcting papers? (There's a large body of research that says youth learn to write best with feedback from peers, not from the teacher!)

* How do students view their homework assignments? Is homework helping them to be excited about learning? reinforcing their self–concept as learners and creators? preparing them adequately for the roles they will take on in the 21st century?

* Is homework building up morale in my classroom or tearing it down?

Classroom Volunteers: Can I get some help?

* What do I need to give up to allow more help in my classroom?

* Can I train parents to do some routine jobs? to work with the students?

* Are there community resources, such as retired teachers, business people, police officers, just waiting to be invited into my classroom for a day or for on–going tasks?

Colleagues: Can we work together better?

* Are there teachers who would like to team with me for certain subjects or certain projects?

* Can we combine or trade so we get more free time, such as combining a class twice a week so we both get one period off once a week?

* Can the principal teach for me once a month for 45 minutes?

Other Areas to Consider:

_____

_____

MORPHING META–AWARENESS

When you teach, what do you think about? What you say to yourself about your teaching and the students' learning is critical. If you'd like to morph an aspect of your teaching, perhaps the first step is to become more aware of your own self–talk. Below is a survey. Write your answers on a separate sheet of paper. Pay attention to your responses and for one month, teach, keeping them in mind. Then take the survey again to see how your inner thoughts have guided you...

Teacher Metacognition Awareness Form

Directions: Answer the questions on "your first impulse." Answer only those questions that make sense to you.

Lesson Preparation:

1. When preparing lessons, do you ask yourself questions about what will or will not work with your students? If yes, write down some examples of the types of questions you ask.

2. Do you rehearse in your mind outcomes of planned lessons? If yes, do you find this strategy useful in your teaching? Why or why not?

3. Have you explained to your students your procedures for lesson preparation? What was their response?

In the Classroom:

1. When you have difficulty focusing on a student's response, what do you do?

2. What do you think about when you are teaching? Does it help or hinder?

3. Do you follow your intuition when you are teaching? How do you know?

4. What makes a lesson work the best? the least?

5. Do you give your students quiet time to think each day?

6. How aware are your students of their own thinking processes?

7. How would you describe yourself as a teacher?

Your Self Care:

1. Do you give yourself time for reflective thought during the course of the work day? Would you like more of it? How can you get it?

2. Would you like to keep a journal if you don't do so already? How can you find the time to do this?

3. What do you say to yourself when you feel your energy draining?

4. What do you say to yourself to restore a sense of equilibrium to your day?

5. Do your students see you modeling self–care practices?

Teacher Morph Tool # 4

RISKS AND UNCERTAINTY

Uncertainty is a fundamental part of reality. This is true at the most microscopic of levels as physicist, Werner Heisenberg demonstrated with his "Uncertainty Principle." If uncertainty is a matter of course for atoms, why is so difficult at times to bring into the classroom? Below are statements that can help determine the role we want risks and uncertainty to play in our classroom. Answer True or False. The more true statements you have, the more comfortable you are with uncertainty and the more comfortable you make your students with it, too! Too many false statements? Try not knowing. The fresh vigor of unfamiliarity and uncertainty will give you an edge!

_____ I can give up control for the outcome of a lesson.

_____ I would rather that a student express original ideas than right answers.

_____ I like when we adopt a curious, questioning attitude in class.

_____ I encourage students to ask questions.

_____ I am comfortable when a student challenges my ideas and opinions.

_____ I can be flexible when it comes to students' interrupting my teaching sequence by taking it in a different direction.

_____ My students feel safe in taking risks in my classroom.

_____ By the end of the year, my students expect to be in uncertainty some of the time during a learning process.

_____ I am not afraid to say, "I don't know" to my students.

_____ I give students support when they are not sure and uncertain.

_____ I assure students regularly that no one has to know all the answers.

_____ I see myself more as a facilitator and less of an expert.

_____ I tell my students how I feel and what I think when I take a risk or move through a time of uncertainty.

Morphing Projects
For the Teacher

1 **Reflect on how the past can help you now.**
What are you getting out of this job? How long have you been teaching: 1–5 years, 6–10?, 10–15, more? In each phase—when was the demarcation that you felt a shift in your teaching? This shift could be either a downward or upward shift—in other words, did you experience a distinct time when you realize that you are giving more than you are getting? Or a distinct time when you gained insight and felt more and more enthused about your teaching? Perhaps you attended a seminar that touched you deeply? Or won a victory at school such as more control of your budget? Pick one positive and one negative experience. Describe how the negative experience was resolved. Describe how you felt about the positive experience. How can you ensure more positive experiences today?

2 **Morph the school environment**
Enlist the entire staff to brainstorm ways to make your school environment more the way you want it. What is needed for everyone to increase enjoyment and satisfaction? Would gourmet coffee help? Would regular flowers in the faculty room be fun? Is it past time for a faculty retreat? Are there any procedures that could be put in place to make someone's life easier. Decide on a time at regular intervals that you could all meet, review your brainstormed list, and evaluate the effectiveness of the changes you made, and decide what the next changes will be.

3 **Do you need time off?**
Why not research a way you can get it? Is there someone you know who could job-share with you if this is a possibility for you? Can you take a year's sabbatical? Are there grants you can apply for? Foundations that could assist you? If you need R&R, don't deny it. Ask for it. Are there colleagues who are willing to take on one or more of your duties, so you don't have to work such long hours? Even if this reprieve is only for a month, how will you make sure you will renew and refresh yourself? Come back to task with full passion and vigor in tact. Now, that's something to look forward to!

4 **How creative are you? Ask your colleagues!**
They will tell you. Together with a group of teachers, make a pact to let each other know how creative you are all, what wonderful teachers you are, and what tremendous gifts you give to your students. So, you don't tell yourself that often enough because you are too busy? Well, let others do it for you! After a period of time, get together and discuss how this has helped. How has your teaching been morphed as a result? What about your enthusiasm for your job? your self-respect? your feelings of being valued and needed?

Chapter 3

MORPHING SELF

In this chapter students explore the process of transforming relationships with themselves. We start with the Self because so often our youth have not reflected upon their own uniqueness and how that uniqueness can effectively express itself in the world. Obviously, their abilities and talents are so needed in today's world, but many have not yet discovered that they have much to contribute. Given the opportunities to explore and examine what lies within themselves, youth can morph aspects of themselves and grow in ways they might not have imagined previously.

The morphing process is one which starts at the micro level of self and continues to encompass and affect larger and larger spheres of influence, moving from the individual, to the community, to the global. Students learn quickly that when participating in a morphing process, on any topic, the self is affected. As students allow the process to work, they experience it as a dynamic interchange. They will soon find that to the degree we contribute to and engage with the morphing process, the process grows us!

In this chapter students have numerous opportunities to understand this dynamic interchange firsthand. Through a rich weaving of activities students can explore and morph issues related to the topics of Knowing Yourself and Health.

Specifically students gain:

*   techniques for understanding the role of self-talk and self-concept in effective solution finding.

*   insight into the ways our expectations, assumptions, and ability to trust create our personal reality.

*   appreciation for the unlimited potential of the human brain.

*   increased understanding of the factors related to health and a healthy lifestyle

Teacher Prep Sheet
Knowing Yourself

Who do I think I am? Who do others think I am? Where do I see myself in the future? What do I need to get there? These are all questions for your students to ponder as you take them through a self–reflective morph. Although there is a level of self–disclosure which happens with any topic in the morphing process, this one is particularly designed to prompt self–understanding. If at all possible, this is the first topic to begin with, for it will open the doors for morphing on deep, personal levels.

So many students have created for themselves a survival personality, putting on defenses and personae just to get along within the system. Using a defense mechanism, such as "being invisible so no one call on me," students can conveniently avoid looking at themselves, owning their strengths, claiming their personal power. During this morph students have safe, varied opportunities to look within and become more aware of who they truly are and who they want to become.

The questions below are designed to open dialogue about self–identity, and provide students with a safe forum for expressing themselves about themselves!

1.   What do we do that we are aware of?

2.   What are many people unaware of about themselves? their actions?

3.   What would you like to be more aware of about yourself?

4.   How do you know when you are trusting your instincts?

5.   Give a story about a time you trusted yourself and that voice inside your head, when others were telling you not to. What happened?

6.   What do you do which helps you like yourself better?

7.   Are you hard on yourself? Why or why not?

8.   What makes you feel special? afraid? courageous? liked? appreciated?

9.   Are you more of a "thinker" or a "feeler?" How do you know?

10. Does responding from your head or from your heart depend upon the situation? Explain.

11. What do you do to treat yourself like a very special person?

12. How are you your own hero?

13. What are your personal goals for the next year? the next five years? the next ten years? the next twenty years?

Teacher Prep Sheet
Continuation Knowing Yourself

14. Describe yourself after you have met the above goals.

15. What is the image of yourself which you carry around inside of you? Does your image of yourself match the image others have of you? Why or why not?

16. Who do you know who are people who take very good care of themselves? What do they do? Would you model them? Why or why not?

17. Do you like to go within yourself? Why or why not?

18. Do you make time for quiet reflection on personal matters each day? Why or why not?

19. What are the advantages of being an introspective person? the disadvantages?

20. Can you be an extrovert and still be introspective? Explain.

21. What do you need to know more about yourself?

22. What changes are you experiencing presently? How will they help you in the future?

23. Do you like to make changes? Why or why not?

24. Do your thoughts control you or do you control your thoughts?

25. How do your thoughts create your reality?

26. Do you believe the saying, "Attitude is everything?" Why or why not?

27. Describe the five most important personality traits a human can have. List them in priority. Why did you choose these particular five?

28. How do you know when you are using your potential?

29. How do you know when you are being true to yourself?

30. How do you recognize and own your own truth?

56

IT'S ALL IN YOUR HEAD

Have you ever really thought about your thoughts?

What's going on inside your head? What do you say to yourself? about yourself? others? school? friends? parents? the future? *your* future?

Thoughts are powerful. In fact, brain research tells us that thoughts are the plastic material upon which we build our entire reality. Some scientists will go so far as to say that **our internal thoughts actually *determine* our external reality.** Not sure how this could be? Why not do the following experiment and see for yourself!

Step I: Keep track of your thoughts.

Watch yourself. What are you saying to yourself? Are you saying that you will fail the test or that you will do your best? Are you saying your parents are all wet or that you can think of a way to better communicate with them?

*   You might want to place your thoughts into one of two categories: Positive or Negative. Are you tearing down or are you building up?

*   At the end of the day assess whether you had mostly positive thoughts or negative thoughts for that day.

*   Think about what thoughts you would have liked to change and go ahead change them—morph them, by just making it so before you go to sleep.

*   Restate the thought in your head exactly the way you would like it, and then, sweet dreams...

Step 2: Keep track of your reality.

What is working in your life? What needs some adjustments?

*   Watch how your thoughts affect your actions. Watch how your thoughts affect how other people respond to you.

*   Pay extra close attention to what happens when you morph a negative thought into a positive one.

*   What happens in your life as you consistently do this for a week or two? What changes are occurring inside yourself?

Morph Tool # 15

Continuation: IT'S ALL IN YOUR HEAD

Step 3: Hold gentle, but firm, conversations with your negative mind.

The negative mind inside us is like a little kid who doesn't have all the information. It needs our help to maintain a positive attitude so it can enjoy life more. And like a child, it needs (and wants) boundaries. When you see that your negative mind is controlling what you think, talk to as you would a child. Here is an example of what you might say:

* OK. I hear that you think I'm going to fail this test because It's the hardest ever. But you are wrong.

* You are forgetting that I know how to relax now when I take a test and you also are not remembering that I have studied a lot. So it is time for you to be quiet and let me take over.

* I know I will do well on the test.

Step 4: Write in your journal frequently about what you are learning as you morph negative thoughts.

This can be a fun discovery about what works best for you in changing your reality. What do you want to happen? Use your thoughts to create the exact life you want... and don't give up—not until you have morphed every negative whisper. Be prepared for many exciting discoveries... about yourself and your new world!

THE HERO WITHIN

Face It or Escape It? Those seem to be the alternatives when faced with a fear, a challenge, or any difficult situation. It's certainly normal to want to run away from problems. To flee when life seems too big to handle. As you get more and more adept at the morphing process, you will find that the minute something is bothering you, even though it may be very painful or disturbing, you be able to come forward with helpful knowledge and solutions that might have eluded you previously. Morphing spurs our ideas and gives us courage!

Take a moment to brainstorm issues in your life that are going on presently that call for you to be courageous:

_____

_____

_____

_____

_____

_____

_____

Now envision the hero inside of you—see this person in as much detail as you can. Perhaps he or she is a strong warrior type, or your hero within is a gentle, but incredibly, wise sage. Think about the qualities of this person and how he or she would morph the difficulties you expressed above. Remember, this hero is a powerful part of you and knows what to do. In the space below write down ideas on how to morph these challenges, reminding yourself that by becoming your own hero, you are becoming a person of courage!

_____

_____

_____

_____

_____

_____

YOUR BRAIN: MIND BOGGLING

The human brain has been called "the 3-pound universe" because if it were making all the connections it were capable of making—guess how many connections that would be?—The number of atoms that exist in the known universe—that's a whole lot of connections!! Most of us use only a fraction of our brain's potential, but it doesn't have to be that way...

Answer the questions below and devise a plan to morph your brain's power...
1. What are my assumptions that hold me back? (Some examples of such assumptions could be: I can't learn easily. I am not an academic. I don't have time to learn anything new.)

_____

_____

_____

2. What are the hidden messages in your assumptions? (For instance, if your assumption is: "I don't have time to learn anything new." Is the hidden message, "I don't find time for new hobbies because I am scared I won't be good at them?"

_____

_____

_____

3. Give three new things that you are willing to try that excite you. Explain how these activities will increase your brain power.

_____

_____

_____

4. Discuss your answers to the above questions with a friend. Remember to explain how you will go about trying the new things you listed, when you plan to do them, and how you will evaluate whether or not you will continue to do them.

_____

_____

_____

TRUSTING YOURSELF

Interview several people. Ask the following questions:

1. How have you been encouraged to trust yourself by your parents? friends? teachers?

2. Who helped you trust yourself the most? What did he or she do that stands out in your mind?

3. Give an example of a time when you trusted yourself. What happened?

4. Give an example of a time when you didn't trust yourself. What happened?

5. How do you know when to trust yourself?

6. Do you feel any bodily sensations when you trust yourself? Explain.

7. How would you define "gut-level feelings?" "instincts?" "intuition?"

8. Does trusting yourself in one instance help you to trust yourself in other circumstances? Explain.

9. What advice would you give to someone wanting to trust themselves more?

10. Does our current society help teens trust themselves? Why or why not?

After you conduct 3–5 interviews, compile your results and share them with your classmates. Discuss the responses, their similarities and differences. Do people in the same age range respond similarly? What do you notice about the responses that will help you trust yourself better? Below, list the five most important things that can assist people in trusting themselves:

_____

_____

_____

_____

How will you use these to help yourself trust yourself?

_____

_____

_____

Morphing Projects
Knowing Yourself

1 **Create "This–is–Your–Life Skits"**
Research the old TV program called, This is Your Life. Study what was done and how the person being honored was treated. Then each member of the class chooses a classmate to honor in a similar way. Gather past data on the person. Find out their present likes and dislikes. Decide who are the important people in his/her life. Then pick a year sometime in the future to look back upon your classmate's past and enact a skit which will surprise them and celebrate their accomplishments. You may want to invite parents to view the skits or include family members in the skits themselves. You could videotape the skits so the person has it all for posterity!

2 **Proclaim Your Individual Strengths.**
As a class you are as strong as the sum total of the individuals in it. Show that you know yourselves by proclaiming your strengths, talents, and abilities. You could list everyone's on posters to hang around the school, you could make up a huge scroll with all classmates' names and attributes listed and read from that scroll to your student body during an assembly especially designed for your important proclamation.

3 **"To Thine Ownself Be True."**
Shakespeare said that. Why not research what other famous people said about the importance of knowing yourself. You could make these quotes available for inspiration to family and friends. Put some in the school newspaper. Read one a day over the intercom during the morning announcements. Choose one to illustrate, write a poem about, or act out.

4 **What Endures?**
Does it matter what you do—the second you do it, it's over. Now that's something to think about. But what does last? What are the traits or characteristics of people that seem to matter over time? What are the surviving qualities of cities, towns, governments, societies? What remains when all else goes? Develop a class list of what endures. Or create a class book, with illustrations or photos of what endures. Explain what will need to endure for a positive, hopeful 21st Century.

Teacher Prep Sheet
Morphing Health

Adolescents view of health in today's world is usually influenced by the images of men and women they see on TV or in the movies. They desire the sleek bodies to feel good about themselves. Yet, many teens buy into the advertising claims that soft drinks will make you popular and a steady diet of pizza and sugar is "normal" for today's teen. Guiding youth through a process whereby they can gain some understanding and control of their own nutritional habits not only helps them develop a health–conscious lifestyle but also gives them powerful tools for dismissing the distorted media images they see everyday.

One activity that might be an interesting way to begin before students pick the topic of their morph is to duplicate a chapter from a variety of books on health, stress, or nutrition. Give one chapter each to a small group for them to read, review, and discuss. Then all the groups share what they have learned from the chapters they have read. This will put a lot of information out on the table and help build a conceptual framework upon which to start. From there, students could choose a critical issue to morph and begin a brainstorming session.

The following questions can spur your students' thinking:

1. Do you know the basics of nutrition? If, not how can you find out?

2. How would you define a healthy person? Are you one? Why or why not?

3. What is your ideal body for a man? a woman?

4. How does how we look influence how we feel about ourselves?

5. What choices do you make about the foods you eat?

6. If you were teaching a young child how to eat right, what would you do?

7. How many calories do you need everyday?

8. What are your favorite physical activities? Why?

9. Are you in the habit of physical exercise everyday? If not, would you like to be?

10. How would you define a "healthy lifestyle?"

11. Who do you know who has a healthy lifestyle? What are they like?

12. Do you think adopting a healthy lifestyle is difficult? Why or why not?

13. Is there someone you lost because of bad health?

Teacher Prep Sheet
Continuation Morphing Health

14. Do you know people with deteriorating health? How have they accepted their situation?

15. Do you know someone who was cured of an "incurable disease?" Tell the story of what happened and your reaction to it.

16. Had you ever had to care for someone extremely ill? What was that like?

17. What do you think of alternative medicine? Have you had first-hand experience with it?

18. Discuss the problems we have within our health care industry. If you were in charge what would you do?

19. Explain the old saying, "Your health is your wealth."

20. What are the best ways to make sure young children grow up healthy?

21. How does stress affect your physical health? What are common sources of stress for you?

22. Discuss your ideal day—a day of a balance between work and play.

23. How can you bring in more real relaxation into your life?

24. Who are competent, productive people who are not stressed out?

25. What is your definition of a "stress-free life?"

YOUR HEALTH: HOW WOULD YOU LIKE TO MORPH IT?

It's been said, "Your health is your wealth" for without health our lives are difficult, indeed. How can you acquire the habits now that will help you stay healthy during the course of a long, productive life? What are things that you could change to adopt a more healthy lifestyle? Do you think you are eating right, getting sufficient exercise, adequate rest, keeping stress at a minimum? Health is usually considered a "state of wholeness and balance." When we are physically, mentally, and emotionally balanced, we are the most healthy. Research about the brain, mind, and body shows that we can no longer distinguish physical from emotional health as the two affect each other so much.

In this project you will have time to think about all aspects of your health and what you can do to become even healthier. You will have the chance to discuss with others how to incorporate healthy habits into your busy day and how to create the vision you have of yourself as a healthy, fit, energetic individual.

Before you start, think of that vision of yourself. What are your fitness goals? Would you like to lose a few pounds or acquire more muscle? Do you want to be a better skier or basketball player? What habits would you like to change? What habits would you like to acquire? Are you too stressed out for your own good? Spend some time thinking about the state of your health and what you want for yourself in the future. Then write a story about your health in the space below:

When I envision myself as a healthy person, here's what I see...

_____

_____

_____

_____

_____

_____

_____

_____

_____

_____

REDUCE STRESS: GO WITHIN

The poet, Eve Merriam, said, "It takes a lot of slow to grow." By that she meant that growth on all levels require that we slow down and enjoy the process of life. You've probably heard of the saying, "Stop and smell the roses." Well, scientists are finding out that if we don't slow down we are much more likely to have high blood pressure, heart attacks, and depressed immune systems. So, how can we slow down when our world seems to keep speeding up? Answer: Go Within

Each day take time to get inside yourself. There are some suggestions below. Try one for a week. Keep a log in your journal, reflecting upon how this silent time is working for you. After the week trial, decide if you want to continue this practice. Explain in your journal the reasons for your decision.

1. At the most convenient time for you, alone in a comfortable position, take the deepest breaths as slowly and as fully as you can. Close your eyes as you breathe and say something to yourself like, "I am relaxed and peaceful." This statement is called a triggering mechanism and as you practice it in this relaxed, quiet time, you will find that you can then say this sentence anywhere and you will start breathing deeply. That's right, even at the beginning of a tough test or in the middle of a difficult conversation with a parent, you will notice yourself calming down. Try it. It works!

2. Before you go to sleep, quietly review the events of your day. Play them through in your head as if you were watching a movie. When you come to something that was particularly stressful or difficult, see yourself reacting in a calm way, even if you had really reacted in a hyped or hasty way. Change the picture. Morph it by visualizing a different, more relaxed picture over it. When you are finished, and right before you go to sleep, say to yourself, "I always react in a calm way in difficult situations." Watch how your attitudes and behaviors change over time!

3. In the midst of a hectic day, sit down somewhere and start breathing and counting very slowly. 1... 2... 3... until you get to 100. Then take five minutes and move in ways that make you feel more relaxed. Sometimes walking very fast around the block is the right antidote. Sometimes just stretching like a cat works great. As you move, though, say something inside yourself like: "I decide how to perceive this situation and I am deciding to perceive it as an opportunity and not as a difficulty."

How do you relax?

Watch TV? Read? Visit with a friend? How about doing nothing?

To get to a place of deep psychological rest, it helps to remove ourselves from having to respond and just spend time with ourselves—without having to do anything. When we take time for this kind of R&R, we find that we are able to handle stress much better. We find ourselves more energetic; more vibrant with zest and creativity. Why? Because taking time to be in silence, we prepare ourselves to receive information, inspiration, and wisdom. This is called taking time for incubation. Our minds and hearts act as incubators of our yet unformed ideas, keeping them safe and helping them take shape in the quietness...

Challenge yourself to be still. How? A good first step is to learn how the environment around you affects your ability to rest. Learn the signals so you can remove yourself from chaotic situations. Look at the list below. Put a check by the ideas that you can try. When you are finished share your responses with friends or family and ask them for support in helping you find more time for deep relaxation and stillness!

_____ Eat lunch a few days a week away from the crowd.

_____ On nice days spend time outside to sit by a favorite tree daydreaming.

_____ Find a personal retreat place in my home if I don't have my own bedroom.

_____ Learn to be comfortable with just staring into space and doing nothing now and then.

_____ Practice sitting, breathing deeply and seeing how long I can stay absolutely still.

_____ Get into a morning or evening routine which incorporates time alone spent inside myself.

_____ When walking down the crowded school hallways concentrate on my breathing and not the noise around me.

_____ Spend more time outdoors, hiking or playing in nature.

Test Stress:

How They Morphed It!

School pressure was big issue for high school students at Beacon Alternative School in Manhattan. As they started narrowing down their concerns they had an immediate mutual pressure which was the SAT tests they were about to take that coming weekend. Consumed with anxiety, fear, and nervousness, they decided to morph their attitude about taking the test. They wanted to alter their perceptions of their fear of failure. The students simulated the minutes before taking the actual test. They practiced deep–breathing techniques to relax, and directed their thoughts in a positive manner, telling themselves this was not a "do or die" situation. They reminded themselves that they could take the test again. They acknowledged within themselves their past performances on tests, remembering that their life and their self–worth could not be measured in one day or from performance on one test. They realized that there were many more ingredients in determining their future school success. The next week, following the dreaded SAT test, the students discussed the value of the practice session and their conscious intent to morph their stress. They all agreed that taking the test, while not easy, was much more manageable. And one young man even admitted to being more nervous during the simulation and morphing process than during the actual test itself!

How we take care of our body is usually determined by how we feel about it. Take this survey and then share your answers with a trusted friend, teacher, or parent. What have you learned about your feelings toward your body? How can you learn to care for your body better? Revisit this survey two or three months from now and see if your answers have changed!

Circle the Appropriate Response:

1. I usually feel good about my body. ....yes .....no .... sometimes

2. My body is as strong as I want it to be. ....yes .....no .... sometimes

3. Emotional distress makes me dislike my body. ....yes .....no .... sometimes

4. I am satisfied with my weight. ....yes .....no .... sometimes

5. I like people to think I look great..yes .....no .... sometimes

6. Exercise makes me feel better about my body. ....yes .....no .... sometimes

7. Fashion models make me dislike my body. ....yes .....no .... sometimes

8. I take drastic measures to stay thin. ....yes .....no .... sometimes

9. Thin people are happy people. ....yes .....no .... sometimes

10. Others' attitudes affect how I feel about my body. ....yes .....no .... sometimes

11. Sports figures make me feel inadequate. ....yes .....no .... sometimes

12. I use diet pills to look better. ....yes .....no .... sometimes

13. I smoke to control my weight...yes .....no .... sometimes

14. How I feel about my body affects my confidence level................yes .....no .... sometimes

15. I enjoy looking at my face in the mirror. ....yes .....no .... sometimes

16. I feel confident when I try on clothes I might buy. ....yes .....no .... sometimes

17. I am satisfied with my appearance. ....yes .....no .... sometimes

18. I compare myself with magazine models. ....yes .....no .... sometimes

19. As I grow older I feel better and better about my body. ....yes .....no .... sometimes

20. When I am critical of my body, I lose confidence in my abilities. . yes .....no .... sometimes

TV BODIES: IMAGE OR HEALTH?

Directions: Below are some questions. Answer each on a separate sheet of paper then discuss them with a classmate or in a small group.

1. Give examples of TV programs which seem to stress that how a person looks is more important than anything else. Do any of these programs promote physical fitness or physical well-being? If so, how do they do that?

2. Give an example of information you learned about health or nutrition from a TV program you've seen recently. Was the program an educational one? Do entertainment programs usually focus more on body image than they do on body health? Why do you think this is so?

3. Can healthy people have a poor body image? Can unhealthy people have a strong body image? Explain.

4. How do commercials promote physical fitness?

5. How do commercials create cultural myths about what women and men should look like?

6. Do TV images of men and women promote stereotypes of larger people? If, so how? Are you biased towards people who are not thin? Is our culture biased towards people who do not fit the media image ideal?

7. What could entertainment programs do to help people develop better health habits? What could they do to emphasize body health over body image?

8. Pretend you are casting a TV program, what would you do to ensure that all body types were represented? How would you go about convincing the producer to include all types of people?

SUGAR BLUES AND FAT FACTS

Fact or Fiction?

Eating sugar will make you depressed. Eating sugar can give you a good energy boost. Fat is bad for you. Some fats are beneficial and actually necessary to burn off fat. These are just a few of the nutritional contradictions we hear almost every day. What's right?

It depends. The question is "What's right for you?" Do you get moody when you eat sugar? Can you tolerate a few potato chips now and then without putting on any extra pounds? Different people respond differently to such culprits as sugar and fat. A lot is determined by genes, ancestry, and body type—some of us are fast burners, some of us burn calories more slowly. The key is knowing what works for you.

Do Some Research...

Some good books on this subject are:

_____   _____

_____   _____

_____   _____

_____   _____

_____   _____

Keep Track of How You Respond...

After eating certain foods, how do you feel? What does it take to feel satisfied? Can you get by with smaller portions? A telling experiment is to write down everything you eat each day for a week. Yes, everything, including any candy bar, soda, or ice cream. Also note the time of day you ate each item. After a week you probably will see a pattern emerging. For instance, it might be that after school, you are so starved you must eat something before you get on the bus or walk home, so a candy bar becomes the quickest fix you can find. If you are aware of these times, you can plan ahead and put an extra piece of fruit or a half sandwich (or both!) in your lunch to eat after school.

Make Changes Slowly...

Good eating habits may take awhile to acquire. Be patient. Take one step at a time. Eat a good breakfast—maybe you'll be able to resist dessert at lunchtime. Some days you may eat more sugar than you'd like. So what? Resolve to do better next time. Remember you are as healthy as your next meal. Bon Appetite!

WHAT'S "HEALTHY?"

What does a healthy person look like? think about? want? This is your chance to create a profile of a healthy person—**YOU**!...

A healthy person looks like... _____

A healthy person spends a lot of time thinking about... _____

A healthy person spends regular time doing... _____

A healthy person chooses... _____

A healthy person knows something about... _____

A healthy person thinks smoking, alcohol, and drugs are..._____

A healthy person usually makes decisions based upon... _____

A healthy person might have the following habits... _____

A healthy person would never... _____

A healthy person is a happy person because... _____

A healthy person can be more productive in life because... _____

A healthy person views the future as... _____

Morphing Projects
Health

1 **Make a Health and Fitness Diary for Today and Tomorrow.**
Choose enough paper to have several pages for a month, several months, or a year. Put in the days and numbers, along with some inspiring quotes from athletes and nutritional experts. Illustrate your diary with drawings, symbols that will help you stay with your goals. Write your goals on the first page and every day, write about what you are doing to move toward them. When you reach one, write in how you feel about achieving that health goal. Then be creative and make up a entries you will be putting in a diary in the year 2015. How old will you be then? How will you be taking care of your health? How will you look back upon the days "of your youth" and how your health habits have changed since then?

2 **Develop a Class Book of Healthy Recipes.**
Adapt or create low-fat, healthy recipes. Just by using veggies instead of meat on pizza and substituting regular cheese with non-fat cheese, a favorite treat can be eaten anytime without guilt. Different members of the class could be responsible for different types of foods. Categorize your book into breakfasts, lunches, dinners, snacks, desserts. Illustrate it and print up lots of copies to use as a fun fund-raiser for your school. Then explain why this will be the most popular recipe book in the next millennium!

3 **Make Health and Nutrition Posters.**
Give the other kids in your school a chance to learn about health and nutrition, too. Make posters which give important information about health and nutrition. Display them prominently in your school lunch room. Talk to the students about them. What have they learned from reading them? Perhaps some other students would like to put what they have learned into a book they make and take home to their parents?

4 **Sponsor a No-TV Week.**
Couch potatoes can't have healthy hearts or lungs—they don't get enough exercise. Encourage physical activity by spearheading a schoolwide TV turn off. Make contracts for parents and kids to sign. Brainstorm all the different types of exercise and movement that could be done during this week. You may want to organize a teacher vs. kids basketball game; a family skating night; a dance; a sock-hop; or an all out track event. Help others become healthy by showing them doing is more important than viewing!

Morphing Projects
Continuation Health

5 **Devise the Standard Nutritional Guidelines for the Year 2015.**
Take a look at the current "nutritional pyramid." Based on your research of nutrition, how will these requirements change? With several other classmates, share your guidelines through a skit. One person could be a doctor or scientist, one a nutritional consultant, a few others could be people interested in changing their eating habits to match what is healthy in the year 2015. A few others might be skeptics and want solid reasons for why they should follow these new guidelines.

6 **Research the quality of the food served for school lunches.**
What are the nutritional components? How do these lunches compare with the U. S. standard of nutritional guidelines? How can the quality, taste, serving size, presentation be improved. Work with the cooks and school administration to work in collaboration for better lunches. Involve local restaurants and interested parents. What can be done to get the lunch you want and deserve?

7 **Morph Stress—Find Private Space**
Make a list of all the places you can go where you can be alone or you just have time to think and be. Because even in a crowded place you can feel alone. Some places might be, library, an empty classroom in school, to the park, a jog around your neighborhood, taking the dog for a walk, going to a museum. Write or discuss the advantages and disadvantages of having a peaceful time by yourself each day. A great book with a lot of ideas about reducing stress is: *Stress–Proofing Your Child* by Sheldon Lewis and Sheila Kay Lewis, Bantam Books, 1996.

8 **Research what it means to be an organ donor.**
Find out how organ donors have morphed the lives of others. Would you choose to be an organ donor? Why or why not? Invite people who have been the recipients of organs to come to your school for a forum to discuss their experiences with you. How has their health changed? How has their life changed? Develop posters, charts, essays, or poems based on all your research explaining the process of organ donation and how this affects the people receiving the organ. Inform parents and community about this gift of life!

Chapter 4

ꟻORPHING IN THE
Classroom Community

The classroom is first and foremost a community—A diverse community of individuals with a great range of skills and talents. How can we better assist students in recognizing their place in that community? In valuing the place of others? In feeling a sense of belonging and personal meaning in their contributions to the community of the classroom? These challenges are on–going, yet the morphing process brings insight and inspiration for teachers and students wanting to tap the full potential of collective abilities to make the classroom a place not only of enthusiastic learning, but also a place for renewal, affirmation, and hope.

In this chapter you will find effective ideas, examples, and suggestions to morph the classroom environment in whatever ways you and your students decide will be most positive and beneficial. As you go through a classroom morph, you may want to emphasize to your students the basic elements of a strong, supportive community:

* *a genuine spirit of inquiry—the basic building block for life–long learning and learning to love life–long learning!*

* *recognition by all that the sum total of the group makes for the gentlest and most effective learning environment. Everyone's contribution is important!*

* *recognition by all that as we build a collective nature in the class we are able to expand our individual consciousness about a given situation. Instead of being stuck in their own thoughts and emotions, the morphing process helps students learn to respect the pull of opposition, and to come to the realization that broadening individual awareness is much more relevant and useful than defending one's point of view.*

* *creative risk–taking skills which increase intrinsic student motivation and involvement in learning. Students know that the classroom community is a safe place to try something new; share from their hearts.*

You will find three specific topics with lots of suggestions adaptable to the varying needs of diverse classroom situations:

1. Classroom Partnerships
to morph procedures and student involvement

2. Friends
to morph relationships for a better understandings of others

3. Peer Pressure
to morph challenging situations in the classroom and beyond

Helping students become aware of and use the power of collaborating with others is one of the main gifts of the morphing process. Traditional schools and classrooms are built on the foundation of competition—for grades, for status within the classroom, for recognition. The bell curve tells students that if one person gets an A, another person's chances for getting an A are reduced. It is a version of scarcity which the students intuitively know to be reductionistic and disempowering. Our aim is, of course, to help students be open, curious, and enthusiastic about as many topics as possible, rather than stressed out, uptight, closed, going only through the motions of learning without any sense of joy or purpose. But how to weave the golden threads of abundance in the classroom—to let our students know that there is plenty of status, recognition to go around; to assure them that an A in a school subject is by no means an accurate or realistic thermometer of their creativity and abilities?

We can change the inherent competitive nature of traditional schooling within our classrooms, and in turn, help students discover more joy in learning, by personalizing the morphing process for them. It's important that they understand that morphing can be done anytime about anything. It is not a rote action or a contrived device to get better grades. It is not a procedure they learn one time and can forget until the teacher brings it up again! Rather, the morphing process is an empowering tool that they can use for the rest of their lives to reach satisfying, creative solutions for a myriad of problems, big and small.

What better way to model the incredible potential of morphing than by using it for classroom issues that the students would like to see changed? In this way they are not only taking dynamic action about things affecting them on a daily basis, but they are also working collaboratively to make these positive changes.

While taking students through a Classroom Morph, you may want to address some of the following with them:

1. Do you feel like your voice is heard in this classroom? Why or why not?
2. Are there people in the class who distract you from getting your work done? How? What could we do about that?
3. Do you like background music when you are doing quiet work? Why or why not?
4. If you could make three changes in this classroom environment, what would they be?
5. Do you think I give too much homework? Why or why not? What would you do if you were me to assure students were learning and retaining information?
6. How do you best learn? How do you know that?
7. What do I do that motivates you?
8. What tasks can the students do to free up my time such as lunch count, taking information to the office, making class bulletin boards, etc.?
9. How would you like to help to make the classroom more of what you want to see?
10. What topics would you like to see covered that are not on the list?
11. Would you like more field trips? Why or why not? Where would you go?

Teacher Prep Sheet
Continuation Classroom Partnerships

12. Would you like more or less small group activities? Why or why not?
13. Do you think we are a community in this classroom? Why or why not?
14. What is a community? Give examples of different types of communities.
15. What are the roles of people in communities? How can being a community help the individual and vice versa?
16. If we were to make our classroom more like a community what would need to be changed?
17. Should parents be more involved in this classroom? Why or why not?
18. If you were to pick the guest lecturers for the year, who would they be?
19. How can our classroom community reach out into our local community?
20. How can we have more fun together?
21. How can we work better together?
22. How can we let everyone in this class know they are appreciated?
23. How do we take what we learn about community in this classroom to our school and become a more cohesive school community?
24. What needs to be done to help you feel like you really belong in our classroom community?
25. How can we best develop our leadership skills in this classroom?

─Lemons Into Lemonade:─

Morphing and Forgiveness

The Morphing of America Youth Film Team was taken to the Presidential Summit in Philadelphia. Our footage included interviews with the president, first lady, Mrs. Gore, Oprah Winfrey, Tom Brokaw, and other dignitaries and celebrities. Inadvertently, through a miscommunication, the bag containing this footage, along with expensive video equipment, was left unattended by several of the youth and it was stolen. Upon this discovery, the adults involved were devastated at the irreplacable loss and had to work very hard to stay open and patient with the youths who exhibited irresponsibility. The youths were feeling terrible about the situation, too. So we decided that the only way to deal respectively with all the individuals was to morph the situation. So we sat in a circle and we let each person express his or her feelings without interruption or comment and we went one by one until all the feelings were vented—the fears, the remorse, the blaming. After one round of listening, we did another. We asked the question: "How can we forgive ourselves and forgive the others involved?" We all listened carefully as each individual answered. Then we did a third round. We each gave ideas about how we can turn lemons into lemonade and morph this situation. We took action in a variety of ways: sending out press releases across the nation to news stations, making a plea to whomever might have found the bag to please return it; filling out a police report; contacting our superiors; investigating who else had footage that we could use for our purposes. Afterwards we listed the lessons we learned individually and collectively from this experience to ensure our growth to be more aware the next time... but most importantly... during this very difficult time we treated each with respect and dignity. The morphing process helped us be more aware of our innate humanity, kept us from nonproductive blaming and moved us to another level of understanding and partnership.

EYE TO EYE

re•spect *tr.v.* means "to look at." Not "to look up to" and not "to look down on." When we look at someone, eye to eye, we acknowledge ourselves as equals who can treat each other in ways we would like to be treated—in respectful ways.

How do we show respect for each other in our classroom? Below is a list of possible ways. Put a check by those that you think you and your classmates are already doing. Leave blank the ones that are not occurring yet.

_____ Listen carefully to others, even when we disagree.

_____ Give eye contact.

_____ Encourage people having a rough time.

_____ Don't interrupt when someone is talking.

_____ Don't talk too much and monopolize the conversation.

_____ Make it a classroom rule not to make fun of others.

_____ Assume everyone is knowledgeable and that their ideas and opinions are necessary to make a great classroom.

_____ Assume we are a classroom of equals.

_____ Expect that everyone is doing the best they can in any given moment.

_____ Keep the classroom clean and conducive to learning.

_____ Both the teacher and the students feel free to say what's on their minds knowing that they will be accepted and respected.

Where are the blanks? Get together with several others and compare responses. Are they the same? Different?

* Discuss your different perceptions of your classroom as a respectful environment.

* Decide what needs to be morphed.

* How will you work together to morph it?

GROUP DYNAMICS

Have you ever noticed that with some people you hang back and are shy or you feel a little bit afraid to be really you? While with others you can relax and be yourself and you don't hold back for fear of being put down? Sometimes just the interactions of the different people in a group can affect how we feel about ourselves.

What about your classroom group dynamics?

* Are there certain people who make it uncomfortable for others? Do some people dominate?

* Are they always answering questions, leaving no space for others to show what they know?

* Have people in your classroom been labeled—the bookworm, or that loud boy, or the nerd, or the giggly girl?

Creating a stereotypical view of others also affects group dynamics—the group can never change if the people are in a little box and aren't allowed to change, either!

Take a good look at the people in your classroom and how they respond to one another. Also, take a good look at yourself and how you aid or hinder the classroom group dynamics. Brainstorm your ideas under the appropriate column.

What I Notice:

About Others in the Classroom   **About Myself**

_____   _____

_____   _____

_____   _____

_____   _____

_____   _____

_____   _____

_____   _____

_____   _____

Morph Tool # 27

Continuation **GROUP DYNAMICS**

Now share your observations with your classmates.

*   What are the commonalities?

*   What are the differences?

On a large chart, brainstorm as a class the problems that occur with the group dynamics. Then on another chart brainstorm a list of possible morphs. For instance, if one of your problems was that a few people dominate class discussions, brainstorm ways you could change that into something more positive, such as having a timekeeper; making sure no one talks out of turn, or stopping a person who goes past time limit.

HOMEWORK HELPERS

OK. You don't understand your math homework. It's 9PM and you left it to the last minute. Who will you get to help you? A parent? An older brother or sister? A friend?

How many times does this happen? That you need help with homework and don't know where to turn? Why not organize a team of homework helpers with your classmates? That way, you can support each other and know that you will be there for each other—especially when there is no one else to help you! Here are some steps you can take:

STEP 1
Discuss specifics with your teacher.
Are there any subjects that are off–limits? Or can you help each other with any homework type and topic? Can you have some time to meet during the class day to work together, ask questions of each other, and plan strategies?

STEP 2
Figure out who will be your helper or helpers.
Will the teacher assign you? Will you draw a name or names out of a hat? Will you have one or more than one helper? Will you have different helpers for different subjects?

STEP 3
Hold an initial meeting with your helper/s.
At the meeting each of you make a list of the ways that you would like to be helped. For instance, one person may say, "I want you to help me with math because it is my weakest subject." Another person may say, "I want you to call me at least once a week to encourage me to plan my studying in advance because I always leave it to the last minute." Basically, find out ways you can be most supportive to one another. Exchange phone numbers.

STEP 4
Call your helper as needed.
Make sure you show appreciation for your helper's ideas, even if you don't use all of them! Remember that you are a team and are helping each other—No one person knows it all, and you know what? They don't have to!

Morphing Projects
Classroom Partnerships

1 **Create a Classroom Morph Suggestion Box.**
Design a special box for your classroom where you put suggestions for classroom morphs. You don't like something? Something is really bugging you? Well, write down the problem, and more than that... Here is the requirement for appropriate use of the suggestion box—along with the stated problem or concern, you must give three possible ways you and your classmates can morph it to a positive solution or change. Take time each day to discuss and take action on a classroom morph.

2 **Create a Classroom Bill of Rights.**
Part of morphing the classroom is to create your own rights: the right to be safe, the right to contribute, the right to be heard, the right to respect. How do you ensure that that happens in your classroom? How can you work as a group in a team to protect the rights of all? Once developed present your Classroom Bill of Rights to others at the school, to family, and friends. Explain your reasons for choosing the ideas you have chosen. Also, tell how you will you use this Bill of Rights to morph classroom difficult situations as they come up.

3 **Research what it would take to become an exchange student.**
First, think about what would be your ideal schooling experience... morph what it would look like. Then pick a few places, other countries, or places in different parts of the nation, or even in your own community.

* Make a list of the resources you would need to transfer schools or to experience a different school in a different situation on a short–term basis. How much money would you need? Do you know people who are exchange students?

* Interview them for ideas and their impressions of the experience. Are there grants, scholarships, or loans for these purposes that you can tap into?

* Work with your school's counseling office, your teacher, parents, and community resources to develop a plan for you to participate in a total new cultural morph by changing schools.

Teacher Prep Sheet
Morphing Relationships with Friends...

For students enduring the emotional ups and downs of the teen years, the challenges of developing and nurturing supportive relationships can be formidable. Yet, youth at this age know intuitively that friends are an "investment" and an important asset. They love talking about their peers. They enjoy participatory activities about personal relationships.

In this morph students both celebrate the importance of friends and explore ways to become better friends themselves. They have the unique opportunity to morph a relationship with a friend or a group of friends within the safety of the classroom environment. During this morph, students may want to discuss the following questions:

1. Describe a friendship with a peer or an adult that has changed over the years. How have you changed as a result of it?

2. It has been said, "A friend is a gift we give ourself." What does this mean to you?

3. What do you value most in a friend? Why?

4. If you were to have the ideal friend, what would this person be like? Describe him or her in as much detail as possible.

5. Explain why you are a good friend.

6. In a technological age, how have friendships changed?

7. Explain the differences in having same sex friends and friends of the opposite sex. How are each important in your life?

8. Do you see your friends as often as you like? Why or why not? What will you do about it?

9. Do you have a pen pal? Explain how that friendship has evolved.

10. Give examples of adults who showed friendship to you? What did they do?

11. How do you show you appreciate your friends?

12. Give advice to friends on how best to communicate.

13. Describe three friends and tell what each symbolizes in your life.

14. Have you ever lost a friend? Explain.

15. Have you met any friends over the Internet? What are the strong points of meeting someone this way? What are the dangers? What do you do to protect yourself?

16. Have you ever answered a personal ad? What happened?

17. How do you know whom you can trust?

18. Have you ever mistrusted a person rightly? wrongly? Explain.

19. How do you keep and build trust with your friends?

20. Do you like to be competitive with your friends? Why or why not?

21. What was a project you did with a friend that was memorable for you? How did the two of you work together?

22. How does having sex change a friendship? Or does it?

23. What do you expect from your friends?

24. What do you expect from yourself as a friend?

25. What do friends make sure they do for their friends?

FUN WITH FRIENDS

Having a good time?

How do you know? What do you look forward to? An important part of being and having friends is just having a good time together. Time spent together which refreshes and renews you both and is not harmful to you or your friend in any way. With a friend, spend some time answering the questions below. Then discuss how you might morph having fun together... What would you change? Do more? Do less? What have you learned about yourself? your friend? by going through this process? Make changes and then check in with each other in a month or so: Are you having more fun? Why or why not?

1. Describe your favorite leisure time activities and why you chose them.

_____

_____

2. What makes up a great time? When you have a great time, how do you know?

_____

_____

3. Is there too much stress in your life? Where is it coming from? Explain.

_____

_____

4. What can your friend do to help you morph your stress?

_____

_____

5. What can you do to learn more types of fun activities? Do you want to learn a new sport, for instance, how can you make time to do it?

_____

_____

6. Are you living your youth? How are you making the best of this time in your life?

_____

_____

GOOD FRIENDS = GOOD MIRRORS

Do opposites attract? Or does like attract like? What way does it work for you with your friends? Do you relish being with someone who shares many of your traits and interests? Or would you rather friends who are very different from you, who challenge you on different levels? Or do you like both kinds of friends?

No matter how alike or different from us, our friends can act as good mirrors, reflecting back to us our ideas, opinions, talents, and interests, helping us to see ourselves in new and different ways.

Take time to consider how friends could be good mirrors.

First, do this simple mirroring activity with a friend.

*   Stand facing each other.

*   One of you starts moving your hands and/or body in a certain way. This person is the leader.

*   The other does exactly the same. This person follows.

*   Continue the movements for as long as you want and notice what happens.

*   After awhile, can you tell the leader from the follower? Who is mirroring whom? What has happened?

Talk about this experience with your partner and/or in a small group. Include in your discussion what it's like to lead or follow a friend, along with how your role changes depending if your friend is the same or different from you. Also share examples of how a friend or friends have mirrored something important for you and what you have learned from the experience. In your examples, were you the leader or the follower? Explain.

After your discussion, use the spaces below to list or sketch ways you mirror and are mirrored by your friends:

My friends mirror me...   I mirror my friends...

Morph Tool # 31

APPRECIATING FRIENDS

You are your own best friend. Do you appreciate yourself enough?

On a separate sheet of paper, write a letter to yourself. Tell yourself what you most appreciate about yourself. List your great qualities, the accomplishments you are most proud of, your many talents. Don't be shy. Tell yourself how much you value yourself. Give examples of the times you pulled through for yourself when the going got rough. Make the letter as long as you want. Include inspiring quotes if you like, pictures that represent important things about yourself. Put the letter and any attachments in an envelope, address it to yourself and give it to your teacher with the instructions to send the letter to you when he or she thinks you would be most appreciative of receiving it. Expect a surprise in the mail! *(Use the space below to outline ideas for your letter.)*

_____

_____

_____

_____

_____

_____

Now, do the same for a friend. Write a letter telling how much you appreciate his/her uniqueness and gift of friendship to you. Include anything with your letter that will help your friend know he/she is valued. Mail the letter when you think it is most appropriate. How was your letter received? *(Use the space below to outline ideas for your letter.)*

_____

_____

_____

_____

_____

_____

Morph Tool # 32

HELPING OUT A FRIEND

* Do you know someone who is considering dropping out of school?

* Have you or any of your friends considering running away?

* When you or a friend are contemplating serious decisions, how might you morph the situation?

Below is a list of some concerns of teens your age. Working with a partner or in a small group, brainstorm and discuss all the possible ways you would help out a friend if he or she had that problem. As you discuss, share your personal experiences to show what is realistic and what's not. Conclude your discussion with drawing up a list of proactive strategies that you could display at your school. You could call it: Friends Helping Friends and under it list all the ideas your group has come up with for helping a friend with a serious concern.

Possible Problems (add any others you can think of)
A young woman is in love with a young man who is jealous and possessive.

Your friend's father is drinking too much and your friend is scared.

You are frightened by your friend's temper.

Your girlfriend has started drinking beer before school each morning.

An acquaintance has invited your friend to a party where you know there will be drugs.

A friend has threatened your other friend with a gun.

An acquaintance brings a knife to school and puts it in your friend's locker.

Two of your friends are starting to hang around people you know to be in a gang.

Your friend has met someone over the Internet and has plans to meet him without telling her parents.

Remember to put this idea on the top of your list:

Call the local teen hotline: _____.

On your list include as many places teens can call to get help.

MORPHING CLIQUES

All schools have them... but maybe everyone would be better off without them. Define a clique. Read the dictionary definition. Ask others for their opinions. Then come up with a definition in your own words:

A clique is... _____

Next, discuss the questions below in a small group:

How do the people feel that don't belong?

What brings people to ostracize others?

Can the cliques change to become more inclusive? How?

How does one go about becoming more popular?

Is it important to have cliques? Do they serve a purpose at your school?

Do you think you are a cliquish person? Why or why not?

How can we see people more with our hearts and less through a filter of stereotyping?

How have cliques hurt you?

How have cliques helped you?

How can teachers support or diffuse the clique–mentality?

Is their peer pressure to join a clique? Why or why not?

How does gossip feed the clique–mentality?

How are cliques like gangs? Unlike gangs?

For this discussion you may want to seat yourself in a circle so that you can all face one another. Use the technique of having the person who is talking hold something special in his or her hands so that the others pay close attention. For instance, the speaker could hold a flat stone, a book, a flower, or any object in your classroom that will signify: When someone holds me—LISTEN. The object is passed to the next person who wants to say something. This is a good way for people to express their ideas and opinions without being interrupted. It helps group members feel safe and can help everyone say what is on their mind without fear of retaliation.

At the end of your discussion, think of a way you can share your ideas with your classmates or your school. Perhaps a skit about cliques performed for the student body is in order?

Morphing Projects
Friends

1 **Letting Friends Go**
Everyone at many junctures throughout life, must say goodbye to a friend—sometimes through death, other times, they might move away; often, we or they just decide that we are no longer going to be as close to each other as we were before and we gradually stop seeing each other. Where are you letting them go to? How can you let people be? And not think something you did is wrong? How do you let go of the good times? Discuss these questions in a small group and develop a list of advice for letting go of friends.

2 **Create a monologue you will deliver to younger children about how to** handle conflict and disagreements with friends. You can make it as serious or as funny as you would like. Think of a time when you had a serious disagreement with a friend. How did you feel? What did you think? What did you do at first? How did you eventually resolve the conflict? Then from your own personal experience, list what worked best for you. How will you adapt this information for younger students? What works best with some friends in some situations won't always work with other friends in other situations. The specifics definitely vary. But there are general actions for handling disagreements without losing friends. Actions that promote caring for the other person while still maintaining your integrity. Include examples so that the younger students will better understand the value of what you are sharing with them.

3 **Create a Tradition of Caring...**
Organize an Annual "Celebrate Friends Day." As a class or a school notify community members, parents, faculty that you would like them to write a short essay, poem, or description of a friend and/or a friend who has done something very special for them. Read through what you have solicited and devise a way to share the thoughts, feelings, and heartfelt expressions in a special way on a day designated to celebrate friends. Perhaps you put the essays together with photos you could take to illustrate the message visually in the form of a photo essay? Or you would like to create short dramatic sketches about the incidents shared? Or you want to morph the essays and poems into a video production? Invite all your family and friends to attend!

Teacher Prep Sheet
Morphing Peer Pressure

Discussing peer pressure with the students may seem threatening to them at first. Some, for instance, won't want to readily admit that peer pressure exists because that acknowledgment would mean they have to face the fact that they are easily persuaded. It might be a painful reminder of a time they caved in. Some, however, will relish discussing this topic. Begin matter–of–factly. Stress that we all experience it in some form or another throughout our lifetimes. That with a caring attitude and effective communication tools towards ourselves and our friends who want to pressure us, we can effectively deal with their pressure and, maybe in the process, still keep their friendship. And when we do, we have morphed the relationship! Taking it to another level of support, appreciation, and deeper understanding. And if we lose the friend because we resisted the pressure than we have gained immeasurably in personal pride and integrity. We have morphed ourselves in profound ways! Below are questions to help students think of a variety of issues related to this topic as they move through the morphing process:

Through this morph, students will recontact their confidence, stamina, and self–respect.

1. Would you rather do something your friend wants you to do, even though you don't really want to do it rather than risking losing your friend? Why or why not?

2. Are you usually a leader or a follower? Explain.

3. How would you rate your refusal skills on a scale of one to ten? Why?

4. What do you most need to learn in order to say, "No thanks." effectively?

5. Describe a situation where you have pressured someone to do something he or she didn't want to do. How did you feel afterwards? What happened to your friendship as a result? What was the reaction of the other person to your pressure?

6. How do you pressure yourself to keep up with your friends?

7. What happens when you are left out of a social event important to you?

8. When are you most susceptible to peer pressure? How do you know this?

9. Describe an experience where you have resisted peer pressure effectively. How did you feel about your decision? What happened to your friendship?

10. How do your parents or other adults pressure you?

11. How does media and advertising pressure you?

12. Is pressure from friends easier or harder to resist than pressure from other sources? Explain.

13. Do some people receive more pressure from friends than other people? If so, describe the characteristics of these people. What makes them so vulnerable?

14. If you were giving a friend advice about how to resist peer pressure, what would you say?

15. What type of person pressures people to do things they don't want to do? Describe their predominant characteristics.

Morph Tool # 34

SELF-TALK THAT HELPS

It's normal to talk to ourselves. We all do it. But sometimes we are not aware of what's going on inside our heads. Sometimes our self-talk gets us into problems because what we are saying to ourselves reduces our effectiveness in a situation.

When we are confronted by a friend and find ourselves in a stressful situation here are some possible self-statements to try. Read them through and then discuss them in a small group or role play a stressful situation with your classmates, while using these self-statements.

	Self-Statements that Harm	**Self-Statements that Help**
Before: **Prepare for the stress**	When I see her, I know she'll just want me to go with her. I always get stressed when he asks me to go out.	When I see her, I'll ask questions about her new house. She loves talking about it and she'll get distracted. I will call up my Resource State.
During: **Meet the stress**	I hate this guy. I'm going to blow any minute. I'll never get rid of her.	As long as I stay cool, I'm in control of the situation. I don't need to prove myself. I know I am competent. I know how to end this conversation.
During: **Cope with Feelings**	I'm sacred to death! Now, I'm really getting mad. I'll show her.	Time to take a deep breath. Inhale calm, exhale fear. Take the issue point by point Muscles are getting tight. Relax and slow things down. She probably wants to make me angry, but I'm going to deal with it constructively.
After: **Release the Stress**	I should have given it to him! I'm still furious. Who does he think he is? That incident leaves me sick to my stomach. I'd better not let my friend see through me.	Forget about it. It's not worth it. Remember to relax. It's better for my health. I'll have the confidence to say something to her. She's my friend and I know she's upset, too.

Which statements would you like to try when confronted with friendly pressure? In your journal write down some that you will try out in your next confrontation with a friend. Reflect upon how they worked for you. Also discuss with your friend his/her reaction to your new way of handling situations. How has that affected your friendship?

YOU'RE THERE... NOW WHAT?

OK... You blew it. You got persuaded to do something, you know wasn't right. You're in it... now how do you get out of it? Sometimes it's very difficult to change, especially when we have to do it quickly because we may be in a dangerous situation. And in the back of our minds, sometimes we are kicking ourselves. All change—no matter what it is—can imply that we didn't know what we were doing in the first place. **OK**—so you made a mistake—the minute you realize that you made a mistake is the minute you can begin a fast morphing process in your head:

* *Brainstorm alternatives—review quickly in your head what you can actually do, given your present situation.*

* Evaluate as many consequences as you can.

* Choose an action.

* Do It!

It's important that you plan ahead and develop safe ways to get out tough situations and practice them. With a partner or in a small group, role play the following scenarios, rehearsing going through each step.

1. You are at a party and you see drugs being passed around. In a moment, they will get to you. You will have to make a choice, what are you going to do?

2. You're friend brings a gun to school and wants you to store it in your locker. You said, "Yes," now you have regrets.

3. You sent a snide letter to a good friend. Now you feel like a fool.

4. Your friend has convinced you not to tell your Dad about the dent you put in his new car when you were out past curfew time.

5. Several friends are getting together to play a nasty trick on a quiet kid at school. You are on your way with them when you have second thoughts.

Morphing Projects
Peer Pressure

1 **It's cool to be you.**
Organize a class skit to show how saying no to a person is showing that it is cool to be an individual and that people who are trying to pressure you are usually not confident and lacking in self–esteem.

2 **Who has the most influence?**
Who has the least? Friends, the media, parents, or yourself? Keep track of the decisions that you make for a week. Notice who you listen to the most, who you listen to the least. What influences do you follow? Which influences lead you to the most happiness?

3 **Set up a Peer Advisory Group for your school.**
This group of students would become informed and learn how best to answer questions relating to drugs, peer pressure, problems with parents, etc. The Advisory Group could put advice in the school newspaper or publish a pamphlet for the student body. They could make morning announcements which include important information and statistics for teens to know. They could hold special after-school events which spark other students/ interest and curiosity. Develop a slogan for your advisory group, such as: Leaders in Action. Develop an Action Plan to accomplish three major tasks throughout the school year.

Morphing Means Becoming More!

Students at a private high school realized that many of them shared the same religious beliefs. When one girl of color was discussing her views about being in the school that had few people of color, she expressed feeling like she didn't belong and was beginning to feel that she had no color. One of the other students hearing this deep, heartfelt revelation made the point that race really went across color and could become religious intolerance as well. From this the students morphed the concepts of prejudice, bias, and racism, realizing that all peoples were linked in a tapestry of similarities. "We all breathe air and bleed red." These new ways of seeing others precipitated by the morphing process inspired the students into more non–judgemental acceptance, solidarity, and joy as a collaborative team.

Chapter 5

MORPHING
in the Content Areas

Integrating a morphing project into a content area can readily assure that inquiry learning and creative group processes with all their benefits are taking place. In this chapter, there are a variety of student activities and suggested projects to act as adjuncts to an already–designed unit of study. They can provide ways to expand an interesting issue and provide you with ideas which can be springboards to you and your students' own ideas for a morphing project, although suggestions for morphing projects are also given.

In this chapter you will find morphing ideas for the following topics in these content areas:

Science
Environmental Issues
Ethics in Science

Language Arts
Symbols and Communication
Transforming Through Writing and Literature

Social Studies
History: Past and Future
Exploring Our Interconnectedness

Visual and Performing Arts

Teacher Prep Sheet
Science/ The Environment

Much of what students hear in the news about the environment is negative. The problems are discussed; the crisis is made clearer and the solutions seldom mentioned or given the same amount of airtime. How do your students experience themselves as change agents for the earth's environment? Do they understand the planet as a living organism? Do they see that the earth can eventually recover from mankind's misuse of its abundant resources and that it is the perpetuation of the human species that is really at stake? Do they understand that any action they take now will have great impact on their future? Do they feel empowered—that their actions have meaning and purpose?

A veteran teacher of fifteen years reports this story in discussing a morph a group of students collaborated on for cleaning up the beach. In asking a fourteen year old year, "What happened to you in this process?" the student replied: "I felt responsible. I wasn't thinking much about that before. But I learned that I care and I do have to do something about it. I also learned that I have good ideas and I can do something about it. You know, I really care about the beach."

Questions to spur student thinking about morphing environmental issues:

1. How do you define environment? Are there distinctions among, local, national, global, the universe?

2. Where does your water, food, clothing come from? Have you ever thought about that?

3. Do you have city water or well water? What's the difference?

4. Does your family have a water filter? Why or why not?

5. What environmental issues have you heard about recently?

6. Were those issues positive or negative? How do you feel about them? Did they give you any ideas? If so what?

7. If you were to pick the top three environmental problems, what would you say they are? Why did you choose them? How would you prioritize them? Why?

8. What is an environmentalist? What do environmentalists do? Do you know any environmentalists? Would you like to be an environmentalist? Why or why not?

9. Do you know any farmers? people working in the lumber business?

10. Does the US have enough land to provide food for other people in the world?

11. Do you feel we have a responsibility to feed the rest of the world? Why or why not?

12. What is your perception of our environmental crisis. For example, an oil spill? or that water's finite? Or that all is interconnected and all affects everything else?

13. Have you thought about how your thoughts could affect the environment?

Teacher Prep Sheet
Science/ The Environment

14. Do you have faith that we can resolve our environmental crisis? Why or why not?

15. Project yourself 15 years in the future. What is the state of our environment?

16. If you needed to, could you survive in an alien environment? How? Explain.

17. Do you think when you do something like recycle a bottle or pick up litter on a street that it will make a difference? Does it seem Mickey–Mouse to you? Do you think it makes a difference? Why or why not? If not, what do you do, can you do, that does make a difference?

18. What would be the most important things to teach your children about taking care of the earth?

19. Will there be stringent rules in the future to protect our environment? If so, what would some of them be?

20. If you were an official for the Environmental Protection Agency, what would you absolutely make sure that the people do? that corporations do? that schools teach? that governments regulate?

THE ENVIRONMENT: WHERE IS IT?

When we talk about the "environmental crisis" or "environmental issues," what do we mean? Is the litter on the sidewalk outside your school? a distant state's water shortage? the nation's air pollution? the world's global population problem? Would it even include the problem of too many satellites hanging out in space?

Answers to the above questions would depend on the answer to this basic question: "How big can we think?" Below are components of the environment in which we live. List as many environmental concerns that you can think of in each category. Then with a partner, answer the questions below:

Your Home   **Your School**   **Your Neighborhood**

_____   _____   _____

_____   _____   _____

_____   _____   _____

_____   _____   _____

Your Town or City   **Our Nation**   **Our World**

_____   _____   _____

_____   _____   _____

_____   _____   _____

_____   _____   _____

1.   Which problems are the same for the "different environments?"

_____

_____

2.   How are problems interrelated? Explain how one problem is affected by another?

_____

_____

Morph Tool # 37

FOR EVERY ACTION...

A law of the physical world is that:
"Every action is a link in the chain of cause–and–effect."

* What do you think this means?

* How can an action be both the effect of previous actions, and the cause of other further actions? Give some examples.

As a result of the actions below, what are some of the possible consequences that could follow? How will those consequences effect the environment?

* tossing a cigarette butt out the window of a car

* taking a shorter shower than usual

* conducting a recycling drive at your school

* running the water as you brush your teeth

* pouring car oil down a city drain

* shopping every weekend

* growing vegetables in a family or community garden

What are some actions you can take to have a positive effect on the environment?

_____

_____

_____

_____

How can you help others help the environment?

_____

_____

_____

_____

Morph Tool # 38

PLANET MORPH

OK You got your wish. You can wave a magic wand and save the planet. You know how to stop the environmental crisis, grow enough food for everyone, clean up the air and water, return rich topsoil to all countries. You also have hired a team of experts in each category to make this all happen.

With a small group, divide several people to work on each area and come up with the ideas, inventions, discoveries that will morph each problem. Brainstorm these ideas on a large chart or poster board. Remember to let all ideas flow, don't censor ANYTHING! Your teams will be brainstorming solutions for the following issues:

*   supplying/growing food for earth's population

*   reducing/educating about overpopulation

*   cleaning up the air, especially in major cities around the globe

*   cleaning up the ocean (You may think that there are several oceans, in fact, you probably learned it that way—but take a look at a globe: Aren't all the "oceans" interconnected?)

*   Returning rich topsoil/minerals to depleted soil

AFTER your brainstorming session, share your ideas with others and add anything else which makes sense.

THEN choose two or three different solutions in each category and ask: "What do I need to know to make that happen?"

RESEARCH in books, magazine articles, newspapers, through interviews, what needs to be known to make your solutions realities.

NOW present your ideas as a team, group, and class in a dramatic, compelling way.

*   Maybe you want to create a planet morph day at your school and present your solutions in songs, artwork, dances, and performances.

*   Maybe you want to create a video about ways to morph Earth and show it on your local cable access stations. (Remember, this is your community station and you can have your video shown to thousands of people, free of charge!)

*   Maybe you want to go into an elementary school and teach younger students what you learned about the vast possibilities for positive change in our environment. See how they would morph the planet.

Whatever you choose—remember, your solutions and your ideas are very powerful. You are creating the future, NOW.

Morphing Projects
Science/The Environment

1 **Ask questions that have never been asked before.**
In this project you develop a list of questions about the environment that are far–out and far–fetched, but which show how the environment of the future will be affected by factors today. For instance your questions might include: How do daydreams affect the environment? If the oceans could talk, what would they say to you? What should be outlawed because of its negative effects on the environment? Spend a few days developing your list of questions. Talk to friends and family and see if they can think of any weird questions. Then get together with several classmates, share your questions and choose some to answer. Brainstorm and discuss your answers. Then put together a project to show the answers. For instance, if you like the questions, "If the oceans talk to you, what would they say?" you could design a skit of a dialogue between a human and the ocean and/or different animals and the ocean talking to one another and in the process coming up with ideas that will make all species and the world's water resource work in harmony for the good of all.

2 **Organize a trip to a recycling center to understand the process of how**
discarded items can be reused and reintroduced back into our lives. How have your attitudes about recycling changed as a result of this trip? How can you change your daily habits to do more recycling? Make up a recycling plan for your classroom, school, or home.

3 **Water, water everywhere.**
There are a lot of environmental issues related to water. Each person in the class could pick a topic to research, then a class collage, mural, or sketch could be created showing how each of these issues can be morphed. In your research, you may also want to find out what is being done or has been done on the issue that is working. Here are some possible topics to consider:

* contamination of water supplies by big corporations

* lead in water pipes

* transfer of animal life and changing habitats in the oceans due to water pollution

* shortage of drinking water in parts of U. S. (or other parts of the world) and piping in water from different locales

* the effectiveness of home water purifiers

* chlorine and fluoride in drinking water

* converting salt water from the ocean to safe drinking water

Morphing Projects
Continuation Science/The Environment

4 Feeding the future population.
Growing and supplying food in the future will be a big challenge. Morphing this situation can be done in a number of ways:

* **Make your own topsoil.** Don't know how? Research and look around in your community. Some places have what they call, "Master Gardening Classes" and teach you how to start with worms and left over food from your table and end up with rich soil for growing nutritious, organic food. Use your soil to cultivate a class or community garden. How will you decide what to grow? How many people will you feed from your garden? Again, look around in your city or town. Are there empty lots for growing vegetables? Will any local businesses help you? What will you do with the food you grow? Give it to shelters? soup kitchens? busy single parents who don't have time to shop? or enjoy all your hard work by eating what you've grown yourself?

* **Calculate how much food will be needed for the world's population in a** certain year in the future. Learn about projection and statistics, learn to read graphs and charts, and consider what is enough food for survival, what is necessary for thriving, and what is too much food for a satisfying life. Morph a diet for an individual or the diet for a population of people. Show how all the people on the planet can eat well, wiping out hunger with the discoveries, ideas, inventions you dared to dream.

* **Reduce junk food and help world hunger.** How are the two related? How does America's fast–food habits use up resources that could be used for food production in other parts of the world? Is it a given that we need the kind of snacks we have available in the U. S.? Morph fast food and snacks. How will Americans eat in the future? Can they eat in a way which will support world hunger, be fun, feel like a treat, and help keep everyone healthy—all at the same time?

* **Research the family farm in the U. S.** Now compare those types of farms with the big agriculture business and commercial farms. Who gives us the healthiest food? Why? How? Should we get back to smaller farms? Is that the best way to feed people? Why or why not? Hold a class debate on this issue and how you will morph it to provide the best environment for growing food and the best delivery system possible. Decide which is best and design a flow chart showing how the food in the future is best grown, supplied, delivered, and marketed. Include the types of food most people will eat, how much and what will be man–made foods in tubes or pills, how much will be altered natural foods such as DNA–enhanced fruits and vegetables, and how much will be purely natural foods. Divide your chart or poster into three columns and list they types you will find in the future in each category, how they are made, processed, and/or grown and why people enjoy eating these types of food. If you will not find that type of food in the future, tell us why. Before starting this project, if your teacher thinks it appropriate, you may want to watch an old science fiction film, *Soylent Green*, to spur discussion of these issues.

Morphing Projects
Continuation Science/The Environment

5 Where is the waste?
Packaging is a big problem for environmentalists because they see that all the waste has only one place to go—back to our Mother Earth. Some materials like plastics take a very long time to break down and become "organic" again. In the meantime, chemicals from these sources contaminate our soil. If reducing waste intrigues you, consider the following issues to morph:

* **Visit a local grocery store and make notes on the packaging of certain** products. For instance, ever notice that cereal boxes are usually bigger than needed? Or that many products come in layers of unnecessary cellophane? Pick one or two products and redesign their packaging. As an art project create more bio–degradable packaging and explain your design and the process you went through with the rest of your class. Then write letters to the companies producing these products, explain that you have an environmentally sound way of marketing their products. Emphasize that it will save the company money in the long run and be so much better for the planet. Request that you be able to present your idea to their Board of Directors. Give reasons why you are making this request. Expect a reply. Keep trying until you get one.

* **What's best—cloth diapers or pampers?** Is throwing out an old lamp more wasteful than throwing out an old pair of jeans? Generate such questions with your class, then decide on a few questions to research. For instance, if you research the diaper question, you will find many viewpoints on the issue. When you are a parent with a baby, how will you decide which will be best for the environment? Make a list of all the possible solutions to the questions you have chosen. What are the best ways to morph waste?

* **Taking out the garbage may seem mundane.** But where does it go after you have "taken it out?" Research where our "throw–outs" end up. What are the negative and positive aspects of that route? If you were to morph how garbage is handled in the future, what would you do? How would you change what is currently being done? A great magazine to read is named, Garbage, and deals with this issue in depth. You and your classmates could read a variety of articles from it, share what you have read with each other, and create a class magazine on "morphing waste in the 21st century." Sell your magazine as a fund–raiser in place of your school's next magazine drive. (How many of those magazines end up in the earth's landfills, anyway?)

* **Visit local toy stores and make a list of all the plastic that you see.** Remember to bring lots of paper as you will probably have a long list. Once children get done playing with all these plastic toys, the toys are usually discarded. Morph this issue for the future. Some questions to consider are: Do children need so many toys? Should toys be plastic? Can we devise ways to give the toys to other children? Can we address the problem of kids not wanting to play with someone else's discarded toy? How does advertisers' ploy of "planned obsolesce" hurt the environment and make this a complex issue? Can children be content with only a few toys? Do children really need

Morphing Projects
Continuation Science/The Environment

toys that change frequently? What were your favorite toys? Which did you have for a long time? Devise a toy of the future that will be appropriate for the child developmentally and that will not harm the environment. Create the toy and give it to a child.

6 **Trading is a way to reuse and recycle and still have the thrill of having** something new. Are there ways you can trade with someone instead of throwing something away? For instance, some goods that can be traded: make–up you are tired of, clothes you have outgrown, sports equipment that you no longer use, pens and pencils cluttering your drawer, videos you no longer watch, CD's or tapes you no longer listen to.

*   Think about all the possibilities of trading.

*   Do some research and you will find that there are communities around the U. S. and Canada that are experimenting with trading goods and services instead of using money. How could this work?

*   Can you set up a place at school where goods are traded? Or goods could be loaned also.

*   If you can create the space or get a business to help you, larger items such as lawn mowers, could be stored and loaned out. Doesn't it seem funny that everyone on your block has their own lawn mower?

*   What if there were a community center for loaning such items? People could have fun working together and reduce the number of lawn mowers and other equipment that will end up in land–fills.

Teacher Prep Sheet
Science/ Ethics

Perhaps the gravest and far–reaching issues of the future will have to do with the increased scientific knowledge and the questions of ethics which accompany that knowledge. With a **morphing project**, students can learn to think of dynamic possibilities and explore a wide variety of options for the future. By taking a current ethical issue in science and morphing it for the future, students are engaged in an interplay of both creative and critical thinking skills while dealing with questions of intrigue and mystery. Even if you are not a science teacher, this section can be incorporated in a social studies or language arts curriculum, as these issues are for all citizens to examine and address.

Below are some questions to use in class discussions
at any time during your morphing project:

1. What is "ethics?" Trace the root of the word, what does it mean?

2. What do you consider to be the greatest scientific ethical issue of the 21st Century? Why?

3. How do ethical issues change based on cultural differences?

4. What recent ethical dilemma have you faced? Explain it.

5. Do feel you are strong enough to stand up for what you believe?

6. Have you ever been in a situation where you had to stand up for your beliefs or been in contact with someone who had a different ethical point of view? What happened?

7. How are ethics formed and upon what are they based?

8. Have you ever been in a situation where your point of view changed and how did you feel?

9. Would you like to be cloned? Why? Why not?

10. Would you like to be frozen for the future? Why would you make this choice?

11. How do you decide where to fund medical research? Is one disease or one issue more important than another? How do you define importance?

12. In the context of medical ethics, how do you define quality of life? Does your age depend on your IQ, age, or social status?

13. Have you ever had to face a medical ethical issues in your family? What happened?

14. Do newer technologies make it difficult to stay ethical? Why or why not?

15. How do you educate people to make ethical decisions? How do you raise future scientists to be ethical?

ETHICS IN SCIENCE: WHAT DOES IT HAVE TO DO WITH YOU?

Choose one of the following scenarios to discuss in a small group. Include answers to the questions below in your discussion.

1. A 15 year old boy has a form of cancer which requires getting radiation treatment. This treatment will most likely make him sterile. He is considering storing his sperm in a sperm bank. How would you advise him?

2. A woman has a deadly disease and without a certain expensive drug she will surely die. However, neither she nor her husband has the money to purchase the drug. So her husband breaks into a pharmacy and steals a year's supply. His wife lives, but he broke the law. Did he do an ethical thing? Why or why not? Was it ethical for the medical community to price the drug so high? Why or why not?

3. A HIV positive, 25 year–old male has intercourse with 65 women over a two–year period. The women were between the ages of 12 and 27. He intentionally did not tell these women that he was HIV positive. A number of women and their children by him are now testing HIV positive. What are the ethics in this situation?

4. A pill, easily acquired, which can sedate someone quickly is bought by an 18 year–old boy. On one occasion he puts it in a 16 year–old girls' soda and when she goes unconscious, he rapes her. On another occasion, he puts it in a 21 year–old women's drink and also rapes her when she passes out. The two women are taking him to court on rape charges. What are the matters to consider in these cases?

5. Sally, age 17, contracts an unknown, rare virus that can be controlled with a certain drug. Without the drug, Sally's health will deteriorate and she will most likely die before the age of 30. Sally, however, refuses to take anything that isn't natural. Her religious beliefs restrict her from taking medical drugs of any kind for any purpose. How do you convince Sally to take the drug? If you were her boyfriend or her mother, how would you feel about her refusing drugs, knowing that her decision can cost her life?

For the example that your group has chosen:

∗   Outline the ethical issues as you see them.

∗   Explain the ethical issues which deal with science.

∗   Explain the ethical issues which deal with personal choice.

∗   Explain what you would do in that situation and why.

CONSIDERING ETHICAL ISSUES

You may know that there are professional scientists, and Ph.D.'s whose job consists solely of reviewing scientific ethical issues and giving their opinions about them to other scientists and government leaders.

Pretend you are such a person. One important aspect of your job is to ask important questions for the future in each case you review.

Below are some ethical issues for you to consider. For each, list possible questions that would be vital to consider for the sake of a positive future. Then discuss your questions with your classmates

Issue: **Questions to Ask About the Future**

Cloning

Cloning animals _____

Cloning humans _____

Cloning only a select group of humans _____

Euthanasia

For the elderly _____

For the sick _____

For children born with birth defects _____

Cryogenics

For anyone _____

For only the very sick _____

Morph Tool # 41

WHO DECIDES?

How will scientific ethical issues be decided in the future?
Who should decide? the government? the people? knowledgeable scientists?

Below are important ethical issues that will likely become more important in the future. Decide who should make the decisions. Give reasons for your choices, discussing them in small groups or with the entire class.

1. Health care costs are skyrocketing. Who will decide who will "qualify" for free or reduced health care?

2. Many natural medicines do the job as well as drugs. The plant, kudzu, for example is used extensively as an astringent to stop bleeding in Japan and China. It grows very fast and is inexpensive to cultivate. Yet, it is not available in the U. S. Who should decide if plants like kudzu can be available to the general public? What factors should be taken into consideration when deciding?

3. Should we be concerned about garbage in space? How many satellites are too many? Who gets to decide? Or should we not regulate this issue?

4. Drivers who use cellar phones are four times more likely to get in an accident than drivers without cell phones. Use of cellular phones has now been linked to brain tumors. Should these phones be regulated? Who would decide?

5. Who decides how a potentially harmful technology is used and brought to the people? For example, it is known that the drug, Thalidomide causes birth defects, yet it is highly potent as an anti-virual agent. As new viruses are becoming more and more drug resistant, who will decide what is safe and what isn't?

Morphing Projects
Science/Ethics

1 **Write an essay about your views of cloning.**
Include what you think to be its positive and/or negative effects. Consider it from religious and social viewpoints. Also discuss what you think some of the medical advantages of cloning might be. Where do you see cloning in the future? Will it be "no big thing" by the year 2015? Explain. To get started, you may want to watch the film, *The Boys from Brazil*, and discuss it with your classmates before writing your essay.

2 **Create a website promoting your school.**
Include school and community events, school activities, homework assignments, information from the PTA, sports scores, student government issues, student essays, poems, and works of art. You could also include teacher and student tips. What are the ethical considerations you will need to make in choosing what to put on the website and what to leave off? Develop a **Statement of Ethics** for your website, why you choose the content that you do and what people need to know about your integrity as website developers.

3 **Research the ethics around a controversial issue and morph your**
research into a summary for your school and/or community. One idea is to trace the origins of the AIDS and ebola viruses. Some researchers think that modern advances in cancer research and genetic biotechnology have given rise to these new viruses. And even more frightening that the AIDS and Ebola epidemics have been planned. One book you will want to include in your research is: Emerging Viruses: AIDS and Ebola, Nature, Accident, Intentional? by Leonard Horowitz. You could use this one book and get most of your information on this subject. Different small groups could read a chapter. The entire class then could summarize your findings and discuss how you would morph this critical issue in the 21st Century!

4 **Hold a community forum on ethical issues.**
Choose a few issues of particular interest to you and your class. Research them and prepare to debate them. Invite parents and community members to a day where you will hold the debates and discussion of the issues. If you live near a University, you may want to invite some scientists or other interested professors. Perhaps they can address the audience, too, and add to your knowledge and questions.

Teacher Prep Sheet
Language Arts/Symbols

Teens are immersed in a symbolic world, very often a world they do not consciously know, but which affects them nonetheless. From fashion designer labels to expensive shoes, the media pushes material possessions as symbols of status and influence. Language, a symbolic system of thought, is another uncharted area. Name–calling, clique or gang names, and labeling others are all ways teens communicate via symbolic expression that goes largely unconscious. A morphing project on symbols could hold great potential for helping students understand the present and future power in representation whether it is through language, art, dance, or personal accessories.

Below are questions to address in the morphing process:

1. What is a symbol? Define it in your own words. Give examples of symbols common in our everyday lives.

2. Can young children understand symbols? Why or why not?

3. What are some prerequisites for understanding symbols?

4. Explain a powerful symbol in your life. What makes it so?

5. Who invents cultural symbols?

6. How do a people agree on the symbolic meaning of an object?

7. Why are symbols important for a family? a democracy? a love affair? a war?

8. Will symbols be more or less important in the 21st Century? Explain.

9. What will be some important symbols for the future? Why did you choose these specific ones?

10. If you had to choose just one symbol, representing your future, what would it be? Why?

11. What symbols are teens most vulnerable to? Why?

12. How does the media promote symbolic thinking? unconscious or conscious symbolic thinking?

13. What are some symbols you know about because you learned them from your family? from the media? from your church? from your school? from your government?

14. Are symbols dangerous? Why or why not?

15. Are symbols necessary? Why or why not?

ACCESSORIES AS SYMBOLS

In the movie, *Steel Magnolias*, Olympia Dukakis remarks: "The difference between us and the animals is that we can accessorize." What did she mean by this?

Think about the accessories you and your friends use; accessories women use, accessories men use in the present day. Think about the types of accessories used in the past that are no longer commonly used. What do the accessories we use to adorn ourselves say about ourselves? How are accessories used to convey symbolic meanings?

Below are some types of present day accessories. Next to each, write what you believe it represents. Think of other accessories and what they could symbolize!

Accessory   **Possible Symbolic Meaning**

earrings _____

nose ring _____

necklaces _____

bracelets _____

hats _____

ankle bracelets _____

scarves _____

_____   _____

_____   _____

_____   _____

_____   _____

_____   _____

_____   _____

What will be some accessories of the future?

Why will people be wearing them? What statements will they be making?

THE SYMBOL OF HERO

What makes a hero a hero? How do people become heroes? Think of someone such as Mother Teresa, Malcolm X, or Alan Ginsberg.

These people are considered heroes by some people, yet their personalities, values, and actions vary. What could they possibly have in common?

Choose a hero whom you admire. Then do some research and answer the following questions about him or her:

1. What is this person's desirable traits? flaws?

_____

2. Who or what is this person's nemesis?

_____

3. What did this person do to reach hero status?

_____

4. Why do you think this person deserves to be considered a hero?

_____

5. Ultimately what does this person symbolize to you? What does he or she symbolize to others?

_____

Now think of someone you know whom you consider a hero. Answer each of the questions above about **that** person.

Use the space below to sketch a picture of each hero.
What do the two hold in common? How they different? Who do you admire more? Why?

WORDS: SYMBOLS OF REALITY

Different cultures think different words are important. For instance, the Eskimo language has 20 different words for the word, snow, to explain it in all its different nuances. Snow is very critical to their lives so they have a lot of words for it. All the different symbols for snow express their reality.

In English, the word "love" has a variety of different meanings, yet it is always the same word.

With a partner brainstorm on a separate sheet of paper all the different ways the word love is used to express all the different types of things people love— such as, I love ice cream; I love my parents, I love reading, etc.

Once you have generated a long list, do the steps below:

Step 1: Categorize the different kinds of love.
For example, if you listed love of pizza, love of chocolate, and love of ice cream—all those could be put under one category, Love of Food.

Step 2: See how many different categories you can come up with.

Step 3: Devise a graphic representation for each particular kind of love in each category. You can make up any symbol you want, except you can't use a heart. (That one has been used before!)
Step 4: With your classmates discuss how your symbols will be used in the future to replace the word love in that particular context.

Something to think about:

There are concepts in our language that have a whole lot of names. For instance, the concept of color must be very important to us. Blue is not just blue. It can be turquoise, navy, sea green, aqua, teal, gray–blue, etc. And of course, red is not just red. It is also cherry, magenta, brick red, etc.

On the other hand, the word love, is well... just love. What do you make of that if words are symbols of reality?

Morphing Projects
Symbols

1 Symbols and Stereotyping

Develop a list of descriptions of a variety of people. Then develop a list of adjectives, such as: strong, spiritual, happy, depressed.

Put the two lists side by side. Now interview people and tell them to link the adjective with the person it most aptly describes. They may protest that this is too hard a task because they can only use one adjective to describe a person and none of the adjectives may be used twice. This is called a "forced choice." After you have gotten responses from about 7–10 people, do you see any patterns emerging? For instance, is the word "strong" used more often to describe a woman or a man? Do most people revert to stereotypical images?

Make a list of the stereotypes you uncover.

* What do stereotypes symbolize? How are people's responses today different from 20 years ago? Will people's responses be different 20 years from now? If so, how?

* What would be needed now to make positive changes in the future?

Present your morphed view of stereotypes and their symbolic meanings to your class or student body. You could do this in the form of a short play, a dance, a debate, or a art piece such as a mural.

2 Architecture and Symbols

Joseph Campbell, noted scholar on myth and symbols said that you can tell a lot about a culture if you study its biggest and most magnificent buildings. Why don't you do just that?

* Research some of the grandest buildings in times past. The Taj Mahal, Pyramids and Temples of ancient Egypt, the Greek Parthenon, the Roman Coliseum and Forum, and Medieval Cathedrals, should be on your list.

* Find out about the purpose of each building related to the time and place and see if what Campbell says is true. What does each building symbolize about that culture and time? Do they represent the society's highest values? Why or why not?

* Now do the same for the present day. Pick some major cities. What are the tallest, grandest buildings? What do they represent in modern times? Are they symbols of what we hold dear?

* What will the grand buildings of the future look like? What values will they reflect? Make a model of one of these buildings and explain to the class what it represents for its time and culture.

* Put your models on display in the school and discuss architecture as symbols for morphing cultural values.

Morphing Projects
Continuation Symbols

3 Get to know other parts of you.
The shadow is a symbol for the parts of us we don't know about or parts we know about but would rather avoid!

∗ Start with interviewing people you know and trust. Ask these questions: "What do you know about me that I don't understand?" "What are the parts of me that are undiscovered that others see and I don't?"

∗ Are there answers resonating within you? Are they telling you something you can use to morph to a new level of self–awareness and insight?

∗ After you have compiled several people's responses, cut out a silhouette of yourself (could be just face or whole body!) from construction paper or poster board. On it, glue a collage of pictures, drawings, photos, that represent what you have learned about yourself in this process.

∗ How has understanding your shadow morphed your understanding of self? Remember this process of self–discovery is a life–long journey where we can use others' feedback to morph personal qualities, tendencies, and habits anytime we want!

4 Create a story in a group and decide how you will convey the story to
another group only through pantomime, without any words! You will need to make up signs and symbols that all will readily understand. And of course you will probably rely on common bodily gestures as a shrug for "I don't know," or a hand wave for, "good–bye." As the group watches, and tries to figure out the story, they list all the symbols used.

∗ Talk about their meanings afterwards.

∗ Then for fun, teach another group in your class some new symbols, such as tapping the feet means, "I'm happy," or wiggling the nose means, "Look at me."

∗ Try these new symbols on people in your class or school who do not know what they mean. How do they react?

∗ Now you are learning how important different body gestures are for people of different cultures. Non–verbal cues are arbitrary.

∗ How will these symbolic forms of communication change in the future? Or will they?

∗ Present a skit showing people from different cultures communicating non–verbally in the future. What has changed from today? What has remained the same?

Teacher Prep Sheet
Writing and Literature

Morphing projects in literature study and writing activities are a natural. Much of the content of literature, for instance, is about change in one form or another. Also, every time we write we are morphing our ideas into the world. Language Arts instruction, then, can be a wonderful entry into the exciting world of the morphing process! Although ideas are as close as a favorite poem, short story, novel, or a journal–writing assignment, this section contains a few morphing tools and suggested projects to help you get started.

Activate students' thinking and creative expression:

1.   What is a great book you have read recently? How has it affected you?

2.   When you are reading for fun, do you choose books that will challenge you in some way? Why or why not?

3.   In morphing to a new level of consciousness, what would be most useful to you? reading or writing poetry? reading or writing essays? Explain.

4.   Who are adults that you know who have learned and grown through the study of literature? Tell their stories.

5.   Do you write in your journal everyday? often? What do you like about it? What do you dislike about it? Can you see any changes in yourself since you started journal writing? What?

6.   Do you remember learning to read or to write? What was that process like for you? How are you different because of these skills?

7.   There are 44 million illiterate adults in the United States. What would you do to morph this situation?

8.   Will the future see more or less illiteracy? Why?

9.   Why is the ability to read and to write well linked to success? How do these skills create capacity for problem–solving?

10. What will the great literature of the 21st Century look like? How will it be delivered? Will books still be available? Explain.

11. If you could meet one great author, who would that be? What would you say to him or her? What would be his/her advice to you?

12. What are common characteristics of popular literature across cultures? What appeals to readers no matter what culture or period of time? Why do you think this is so?

13. How would you advise people who say that they don't have time to read?

14. How can you use your writing skills to morph important issues right now?

15. Describe your reading and writing skills in the year 2020.

WHO ARE YOU? WHO WILL YOU BE?

Write a poem about yourself in the past.

Pretend you are you in the future year of 2015. How old will you be then? Who are you now? Use the following sentence frames to construct your poem.

I used to be... but now I am...

Some see me as... but I really am...

People thought me to be... but I am sure I am...

I used to like... but now I like...

I used to believe... but now I believe...

My friends were... but now they are...

I used to value... but now I...

I wanted so much to... and now I realize that...

I used to be... but now I am...

Use the space below to craft your poem.

Change lines, add lines, polish it the way you want it. Then share it with your classmates. Role–play a class reunion. It is the year 2015. Greet old friends. Tell them about yourself. Who are you now?

_____

_____

_____

_____

_____

_____

_____

_____

MORPHING PSYCHOLOGICAL PATTERNS

The newspapers abound with high drama depicting many of the same patterns of human behavior which have been immortalized in myths and fables. Some are:

* How ego and pride can be a person's downfall

* Disloyalties and betrayals

* Infidelities

* Wars

* Trickery or fraud

* Children being given elsewhere to be raised

What are some other themes, or archetypal, psychological patterns common to the human condition? Brainstorm some with your class or in a small group:

_____   _____

_____   _____

_____   _____

_____   _____

_____   _____

_____   _____

1. Choose a newspaper article that depicts one of the common psychological patterns listed above.

2. Research a myth or fable which best illustrates the human behaviors found in your newspaper article.

3. Now morph your newspaper article by writing a modern–day myth or fable . You can use the already existing myth you found as a model. But be sure to change names, and make the setting, time, and place in the present. You may give a moral of your new myth, if you like.

4. Share your myths or fables with your class. Discuss the following questions:

* How can these psychological patterns be morphed in the future?
* If we were writing a future myth, how would it change? How would it be the same?

Morph Tool # 47

WHAT'S GOING ON INSIDE?

Read a literature selection in which what the person is thinking is different from what he or she is actually saying. A good example is the short story by Dorothy Parker, entitled, "The Waltz." As two people dance, the woman makes pleasing statements to her partner, while she is thinking how terrible it is to be dancing with him. The result is humorous because much of humor is based on the difference between what is said and what is thought about what is said.

After you have read your selection, think about how you can morph an issue important to you using the same type of technique.

* You can write a story, essay, song, poem, or play where you depict the difference between what is said (the external elements) and what is thought (the internal elements).

* Make your writing as humorous as you would like and at the same time convey a serious message for the reader.

* Then present your morph to the class in an interesting, unique way.

When you are finished evaluate your own writing and have someone else give you feedback, too. You can use the form below. *On a scale of 1 –5, with 5 being the highest, rate your creation on the following criteria:*

	Your Rating	Someone Else's Rating
Originality, Creativity	_____	_____
Clarity of thinking	_____	_____
Humor	_____	_____
Message conveyed	_____	_____
Vocabulary, word choice	_____	_____
Spelling, grammar	_____	_____
Any other categories you want to evaluate?	_____	_____

120

Morphing Projects
Writing and Literature

1 **Challenge yourself to read two books a week (or two books a month!).** The books can be long or short, but should be at a level you can read fairly easily. How to find the time? Watch less TV. Play less video games. Organize a reading time with your friends where you all get together with friends. Bring food, and share what you have read with one another after an hour of silently reading together. This works well if you are all reading the same book for school. Ask your teacher for a list of short books with education and entertainment value. Read two books a week for two or three months. Then see how you have changed.

* How have you morphed your academic success?

* Is all that reading paying off?

* Do you answer more in class discussions?

* Do your teachers notice you using a wider range of vocabulary in your written work?

* How have you and your skills been morphed as result of this experiment?

2 **Choose one of your favorite books, articles, poems, recipes, or songs and lend** it to someone to read. Do the same with someone. Talk about it together. Discuss how it has affected your outlook and how its contents might affect you in the future. How does literature morph our perceptions? attitudes? values?

3 **Hold a poetry reading or organize regular poetry readings once a month.** Encourage anyone who has written a poem to attend and share it with others. You may want to feature a particular, favorite poet, living or dead, and read from his or her works, too. After the readings, discuss the value of incorporating more poetry into our future society.

* Would we benefit from more?

* Or do we have enough poetry?

* List the ways we get exposed to poetry from music to ads to children's books.

* Are there other ways you would include in the future?

* Why would access to poetry be important to the future?

Teacher Prep Sheet
Social Studies: Past/Future

The Morphing Process, by its very nature, links the past with the future. In fact, whenever we envision a goal or an image, we rely on past knowledge and past experience to do so. As you take students through a Past/Future morphing project, it might be interesting to point out this fact to them and ask them to consider how their past is influencing what they anticipate or want for their future. Adding this metacognitive component throughout will also help students see the relevance of the morphing process beyond school assignments and classroom projects.

Some other questions you can ask your students
throughout this morphing project are:

1. If you could rewrite any portion of past world history, what would it be? How would you rewrite it? Why did you choose this part of history to rewrite?

2. Give examples of how the past determines a person's future.

3. Who do you know who has overcome difficulties in their past to create a successful life? Tell their story. Is it inspiring to you? Why or why not?

4. Do you think that even the little decisions we make every day will influence the future in a big way? Explain.

5. How can we use the past to morph the future?

6. Choose a great leader from the past and explain how he or she would lead today. Would this person be effective? Why or why not? What demands, pressures are different today? What are the same as the past? How would he or she have to change to be a great leader today?

7. It has been said, "If you don't understand history, you are doomed to repeat it." What does this mean to you personally? What could it mean for an entire culture?

8. What have you learned in the past that you were sure to carry over to your future? How has that worked for you? Explain.

9. Pretend you can see into the future. What are the significant events taking place now that have influenced the future?

10. What are characteristics of people, societies, and civilizations that span time? Qualities that endure over time? How do these qualities stay alive over time?

DOES HISTORY REPEAT ITSELF?

It has been said, "Those that do not understand history are doomed to repeat it."
Are we repeating a past and are unaware of it?

With a partner take a close look at the past civilization of Rome, right before its fall.
Examine some of the causes for that fall, and place a check by the ones that seem
pertinent to America today. What are the parallels found in today's society?

Some Causes for the Fall of the Roman Empire:

* big gap between rich and poor

* much of the capital and property in the hands of the rich

* the empire was consuming more than it was producing

* the people were entertaining themselves more than working

* the tax structure was such that those who were most able to pay were taxed the least;
  those who couldn't pay, were taxed the most

* people loved violent forms of entertainment; entertainment kept getting more and
  more violent

* violent entertainment was a way to assuage the people's anger at their poor living
  conditions

* cities were overcrowded resulting in squalid landlord housing

What do we have to do to prevent history from repeating itself?
Take one of those issues and brainstorm ways to morph it in such a way that it won't
lead to repeating the same disaster.

List some positive steps individuals or society can take:

_____   _____

_____   _____

_____   _____

_____   _____

_____   _____

MAINTAINING DEMOCRACY

What are the elements necessary for a democracy to exist and perpetuate?
Some are:

*   Participation of the people

*   Education

*   People must have their basic needs met so they have time and energy to look beyond themselves and to the group as a whole

*   freedom of expression

Can you think of any other important elements?
Now... Research two countries—the United States and another country that doesn't have a democracy. In your explorations compare the following between the two countries:

*   Percentage of people voting

*   Statistics on literacy

*   Infant mortality rate

*   Gross national product

*   Life expectancy

If these are strong factors in developing a democracy? Where are we? How do we compare with the other country you have chosen?

Next... Consider where each country will be in the future. Pick several of the above issues and show how they can be morphed to help create a brighter future for each country. You can continue your research and...

Take one of the issues such as literacy or number of people that vote and research why this particular issue is such a problem in the US.
Then do a service project in your school or community about it. For instance, you could devise and print a pamphlet about the importance of voting, bring political candidates to the school to talk with you and your parents, organize a mock vote at your school during a state or national election, go around your neighborhood and encourage people to register to vote, if they are not already registered. Start morphing now to maintain our democracy in the future!

EVENTS MORPH US!

What happens in the past affects us!
The more significant the event, the more significant the effect!

In a small group, brainstorm significant events or discoveries that changed the world and led to a sequence of events that affected you! Some examples are: the discovery of fire, agriculture, the inventions of the automobile, penicillin, and television!

After you have a list, pick one invention or discovery, research it to find out the linkages about how it infused and changed society. List as many ways as possible. Spend some time on this and think through the far-reaching effects of the invention or discovery.

Then each small group should illustrate or find a picture of the invention or discovery researched, along with pictures showing some of the effects or changes it made. For instance, if your discovery is fire, a far-reaching effect is the modern-day oven.

Now the entire class can create a timeline showing inventions, discoveries, and their long-range effects.

* Get together and decide on the time span of your timeline and where in your class or school you will create it.

* Consider how you will show which effects are related to a specific invention or discovery.

* One idea is to put your pictures on the timeline with different colors of background paper which would relate to specific inventions or discoveries and their effects. The effects of one invention or discovery and its specific effect would all be the same color.

* You decide what will work best to show how the past has morphed the future!

When you have your timeline complete. Look at it as a class, spend time reflecting on it and discuss how all the events, invention, and discoveries have morphed our present reality and how they have effected us as individuals and as a society.

For More Morphing Fun...
Consider: What will be invented or discovered in the future that will have significant effects? Create it. Or draw it. Or write about it. Make a future timeline. How has the future been morphed?

A FUTURE SPEECH

Choose a speech from a famous person of the past that had an effect on people. Some examples include:

* Franklin Roosevelt—fireside chats
* Winston Churchill on World War II
* Chief Seattle on the environment
* John Kennedy's inaugural speech
* Caesar Chavez on farmworkers
* Harriet Tubman on slavery
* Simone deBeavior on women's freedom
* Gertrude Stein on cubism in art
* Gloria Steinem on women's rights

Read the speech and discuss with your classmates the reasons it was such an effective speech. What were the elements in it that made it so memorable?

List some of them below:

_____

_____

_____

Pick a portion of the speech or the entire speech and rewrite it as if that person were giving that speech in the future in the year 2010. What would change, what would stay the same? How will the person's speech affect people in the year 2010?

_____

_____

_____

Practice your new speech and deliver it with expression and enthusiasm to your classmates. Get their feedback. How was the speech received? Did it move people to take action on the issue?

Tape record your speech and put in it a special place where you will remember to listen to it in the year 2010!

Morphing Projects
Past/Future

1 **Write a Future Diary of an Explorer, Traveler, or Historian.** First research and read some diaries of people who commented on their times, either non–fiction or fiction. Some examples might be: *Diary of Anne Frank*, Civil War or World War I or II letters, Admiral Perry's letters about the North Pole, *Travels with Charley* by John Steinbeck, or *On the Road* with Jack Kerouac. Why are they interesting? What are the commonalties? Pick one example and examine it in more depth:

* What aspects are similar to aspects of today? What aspects are different?

* Now write a future diary of someone who has explored or lived through an historical event. Enter a week's worth of daily thoughts and activities.

You might also want to consider:

* What are the qualities of being a great adventurer?

* What qualities from past explorers need to be brought forward into the future?

2 **Choose an historical event from the past, such as World War II.** Rewrite history. For instance, what if Hitler had won? How would our lives be different today? How would this personally affect you, your family, friends, local and national government?

3 **Traditions: Bridge between past and future.** Are you carrying the past with you? In some ways we all do when we have family or cultural traditions which have been handed down to us from our ancestors. Think about the future of traditions. What would be a future without traditions?. Imagine your family life in the year 2020—what are the traditions you are teaching to your children? Design these future traditions and present them to your class and/or student body. Explain how and why you have morphed the traditions.

Morphing Projects
Past/Future

4 **Choose a great leader or personality from the past.** Write an essay, story, or poem on how this person would be an effective leader or influential person in the future. Some names to consider are: Thomas Jefferson, Harriet Tubman, Abraham Lincoln, Gandhi, Eleanor Roosevelt, or Winston Churchill.

5 **Interview people, age 50 or older, and discuss how the past, from their** perspectives, have influenced the present. Then discuss their opinions about what the future will be like. Compare their ideas with people your own age. Does knowing more about the past, give people an edge in anticipating the future? Do the older people give you any more insights than the younger ones? Is past experience important for understanding and coping with the future? Make up a chart with the ages of the people you interviewed, some of the questions asked, and their responses. Graphically display your information. Share it with your class or student body. Discuss how to morph the future by understanding the past!

Teacher Prep Sheet
Social Studies: Interconnectedness

A veteran teacher with fifteen years experience found that her students thoroughly enjoyed their morphing project. She commented, "Not only does it help them understand the interconnectedness of all peoples, morphing is connecting them to everything they are." You will find that in many morphing projects, the concept of interconnectedness naturally comes up to be explored, discussed, and, eventually, morphed—resulting in the natural progression of this process—the experience of being more deeply connected to oneself.

Since the theme of interconnectedness permeates morphing, it can be emphasized within any content area or critical issue chosen. For instance, even as a social studies teacher, you may want to refer to the environmental morphing ideas in the science section which can be easily adapted to a social studies unit on interconnectedness. In fact, many of the topics covered in this book, can be adapted for a morph focusing on interconnectedness!

As you explore this topic with your students, here are questions to discuss:

1. What does it mean "to be a part of the whole?" to "contribute to the whole?"

2. How do you feel connected to others? to your family? to your school? to your community? to the world?

3. Do you think computer technologies have made people feel more or less connected with each other? Explain.

4. How does trade among nations reflect their interconnectedness?

5. Do you trade with others? How is this worked out? How does everyone benefit?

6. Is it important to feel connected and important to others? Why or why not?

7. How will third world nations become more connected to industrial nations in the future?

8. How does experiencing our interconnectedness make us more compassionate?

9. Who are people that you know who honor the concept of interconnectedness in their daily lives? What are their qualities and characteristics?

10. What are ways that do not exist today that people will experience their interconnectedness in the future?

11. How does interconnectedness between and among nations increase the need for collaboration and negotiating skills?

12. Give an example from your own life when you deeply felt your interconnectedness with others or with the planet. What happened as a result of this experience?

Morph Tool # 52

WHERE DID IT COME FROM?

Sometimes it is not real obvious that we, the people of the United States, are connected to and rely on people from other parts of the world.

Morph your awareness of our interconnectedness by doing the activity below:

Step 1: Choose a common, everyday object, such as a shoe, a calculator, or even a candy bar.

Step 2: Research the origins of every part of that object. For instance, if you researched a candy bar, you would have found out that the foil wrapping it has some aluminum in it, that aluminum comes from bauxite, and that bauxite is mined in Surinam. You would realize that the chocolate comes from Central America co-co beans. Where did the sugar cane for the caramel come from? Where was the candy made? Where was the wrapper printed?

Step 3: After you have found out the origins of every possible part of your object, construct a display. Take a large piece of poster board, place your object in the center. Then use different colored strings radiating out from the center object to connect with all the other parts and their origins. Your display might look something like this:

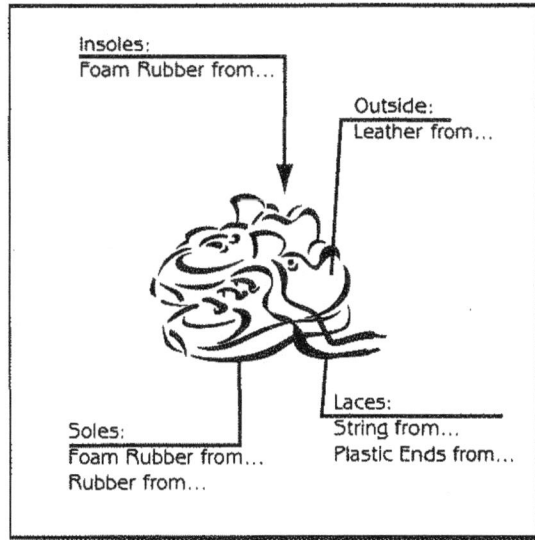

Step 4: Present your findings to the class and discuss all the ways various objects and places are interconnected. Include these questions in your discussion:

*   How will this interconnectedness change in the future?

*   Were you surprised about any of the connections?

*   Would you change any of the connections? If so, why?

MORPHING CONNECTIONS

To learn social studies well, it also means learning new terms and vocabulary.

* How do you study to retain these words?

* Do you find the work boring and tedious?

Below is an alternate activity to do with a small group. It will be a fun way to experience the interconnectedness among many meanings and discover a unique memory devise!

As a class...
Write vocabulary terms on 3x5 cards. One word to a card. Make up about 100 cards. Shuffle the cards and distribute 20 cards to each group.

In your groups...
Make up four different categories and place each word in a specific category. For instance, you could have regular–type categories, such as, "significant events," or "great leaders," or you could have far–out categories, such as, " words beginning with b," or "terms longer than 8 letters." Each person in the group, then takes a turn, putting a word under an existing category. They may ask other students for assistance, or other students may ask questions about their thinking on where they placed their card. The final decision, however, is up to the person who holds the card. When everyone's cards are placed, glue them under the categories on a poster board.

Back to the whole class...
Each group presents their words and categories to the rest of the class, explaining why they decided to put the term under that specific category. Students question and debate about category placement. How does the category placement morph the definition of the word? How does the category placement morph the ways the words and their definition are interrelated? Reflect on others' points of view? How are different ideas connected with each other? How do varying opinions about category placement show interconnectedness?

Use can Morph Word Connections like this when you are studying for a test! By putting words into categories and debating them with friends, you are going to remember these words and their definitions for a long, long time!

Morphing Projects
Exploring Our Interconnectedness

1 **Pick a country.**
Now pick another country. Research their relationship. Are they friends? foes? Do they trade with one another? Why or why not? What do the people think of each other? Can they travel freely in each other's countries? Are they first, second, or third world countries? Now show what their relationship will be like in the future. How has their relationship morphed? How will you show that change?

2 **Show the interrelatedness of all the activities of a political campaign.**
Collect information such as how much money it costs to run for office, what are the procedures for filing, how do candidates interview and choose people to work for them, what kinds of decisions must be made about media ads. Gather information from booklets, videos, newspapers, interviews of political candidates. Once you have as much information as you can get, conduct a simulated political campaign. Different groups can develop and role–play the following: A poster, a speech, a radio commercial, a Public Service Announcement for TV, a web page. Analyze the elements of political campaigns that are currently working, pick elements that need changing; those that could be adjusted to work better. Also identify practices that definitely need to be eliminated. Then: organize a class writing campaign to the president, or state, or local politicians. In your letter include some of your concerns, what you have found out through your research, and what you think should be done to improve the country's state, or local campaign system. Invite the politicians, along with the press, to a special day at school where you will share the ways political campaigns could be morphed in the future.

3 **Write a one–page story about the leadership skills necessary in the 21st century.**
Do not put your name on your paper. Take a few days to develop your story to ensure quality and completeness. Have your teacher pass out the stories when everyone has finished. Read the anonymous story you have gotten. Then list the characteristics of the type of person who could have written this story. Guess which one of your classmates wrote it. Discuss the interrelatedness between personal characteristics and leadership skills important in the future. What are the connections between:

*   personal characteristics and leadership ideas?

*   personal values and values about leadership?

Morph your stories into a short play or sketch for your school. Show how the leaders of the future will be effective. Invite the audience to discuss your play and their ideas about future leadership after the presentation.

Teacher Prep Sheet
Visual and Performing Arts

A friend, on return from a trip to Canada, remarked: "What stands out in my mind the most, is seeing so many children and teens drawing in their free time. And not for school assignments, either! For instance, walking through parks, kids from about ten through 17, had easels set up and they were sketching. In three different parks, I encountered a total of 20 kids! When I inquired about what they were doing—all of them responded with dignity and pride in their work and all of them, and this is the amazing thing, said they were doing it, "just for the fun of it." It's so sad for me to think that in all my 55 years I have never encountered anyone under 17 in the U. S. sketching in a park on a warm spring day, "just for the fun of it."

How many of our students see themselves as artists? as crafters? as performers? How many are in touch with their unique, creative self–expression? Since the arts are usually the first cut–backs made when budgets get tight, too often students enter junior high or high school with limited experience in artistic endeavors. Since, students don't readily see themselves as artists, they don't often select art electives and, many times, only choose those classes as "fillers." Not taking art seriously means not understanding the value of art education.

The arts, as avenues of original expression, are also doors to impactful morphing projects. By discovering and practicing their own unique expression in the visual and performing arts, students can gain valuable insights into their own magnificent capacity for creative solution finding. A morphing project in the arts can also assist students in comprehending the integral value of art education for everyday life. Students are immersed and engaged in a transformational process which awakens and alivens latent creative talent. Since morphing can easily lead to a myriad of artistic expressions, teachers of content areas are encouraged to use this section, also. It is not only for art and drama teachers! You will find plenty of ideas which can be adapted for any content area, ensuring that the students experience a wide variety of artistic expressions in the morphing of any issue!

Below are questions
which will help students engage more fully with artistic, creative expression throughout a morph:

1. When was the last time you drew, used crayons or colored pencils, or painted, "just for the fun of it?"

2. Compare your early childhood experiences in art and drama with those of today.

3. Who is an artist that you know? What are the qualities that you admire in him or her?

4. Are art and artists appreciated in our culture? Why or why not? How do you know?

Teacher Prep Sheet
Continuation Visual and Performing Arts

5. What type of art—drawing, painting, performing, playing a musical instrument—would you like to learn or refine? How can you go about doing this? What will need to be morphed in your life in order to do it?

6. What do you think this quote by Julia Cameron, author of *The Artists' Way,* means? "Creativity lives in paradox: serious art is born from serious play."

7. Do you play enough? How do you know?

8. Give advice to a friend wanting to pursue a career in the arts. What will she/he need to do?

9. Do you think professional artists should be paid as well as professional athletes? Why or why not?

10. What modern day plays, songs, pieces of sculpture, drawings, artwork will be available for people to enjoy in the year 2020? What qualities make these so enduring?

Morphing:

Becoming Responsible Creators

A 6th and 7th grade art class formed five different groups to morph five critical issues: time, racism, cleaning up the environment, self–esteem, values and morals. They studied various approaches to drawing and painting and their final pictures depicted how they would morph their particular issues. Not only did they learn and practice artistic techniques, but they learned much about themselves as responsible creators. One girl, for instance, realized that she had been unaware of the litter and mess in her environment. She vowed that for the rest of her life she would do her part to help keep the environment clean. Even weeks after this morphing project, she revealed that she finds herself more involved, more caring. When noticing that a parking meter had run out and the driver was nowhere to be seen, she put a dime in the meter. Morphing means responsibly creating an environment of caring.

COOPERATIVE MORPHING!

With two other students, extend the segments of the three drawings below toward the center of the page. But NO TALKING! Can the three of you form one, recognizable image? Watch what you are saying to yourself as you work together. Discuss your experience of this process with each other when you are finished.

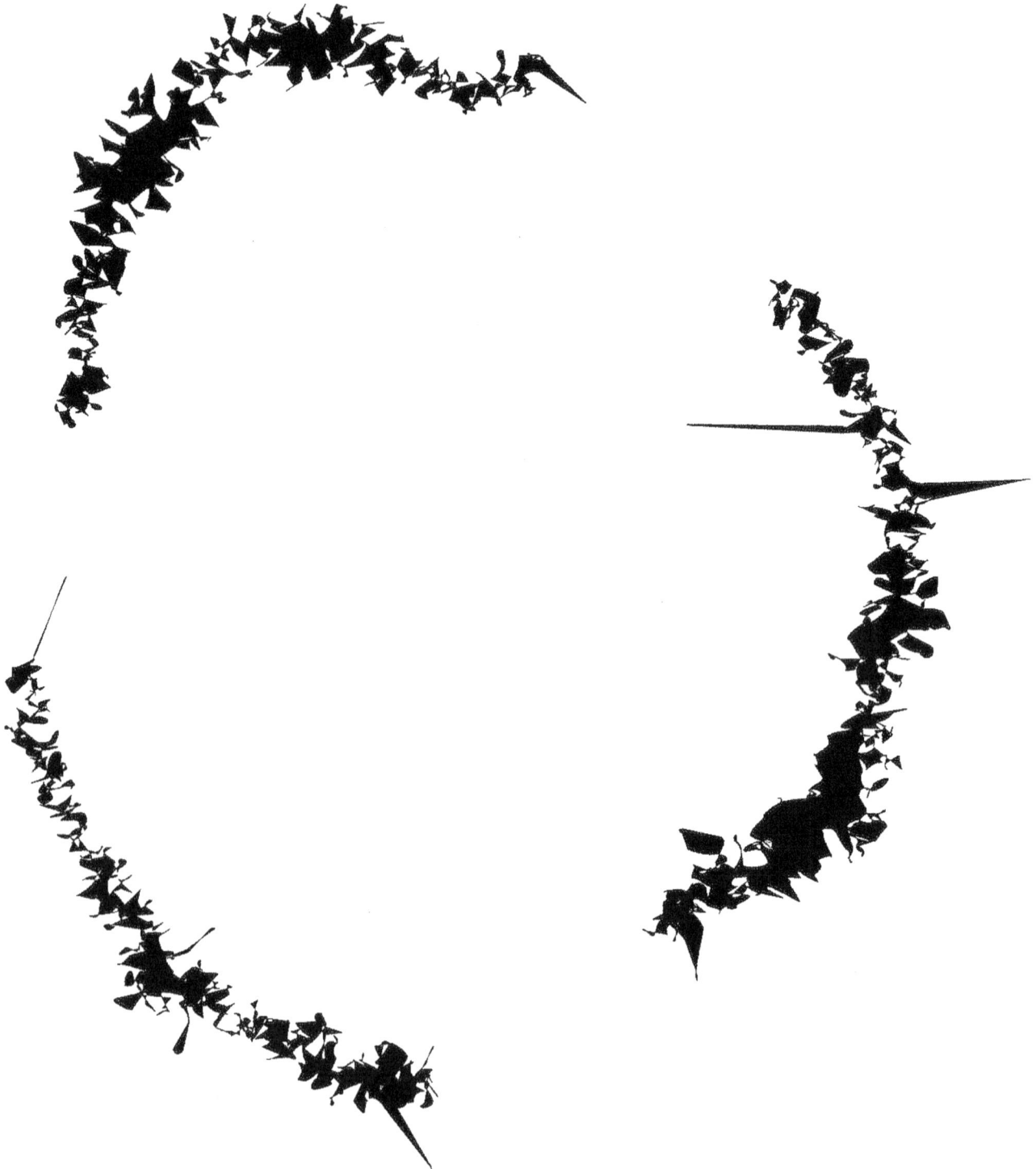

Morph Tool # 55

FROM IMPROV TO SCRIPT

Once you have decided on a critical issue to morph, you can go through the process below to design a performance piece.

Step 1: In a group of four, speaking extemporaneously with each other on the issue from various points of view. For instance, if your issue to morph is air pollution, take turns speaking from the following perspectives: an environmentalist, a chemical corporation executive, a scientist specializing in the ozone layer, the CEO of an automobile company. It might help to tape record or video tape these improvs for future reference.

Step 2: Discuss all the points of view expressed and synthesize them into one overview. Group members (or the class) agree on one point of view about your critical issue. This is the point of view you will be perpetuating in your play or sketch.

Step 3: Decide on the sequence of ideas that will develop the strong message and point of view you want to get across. Will you include dance? What music will fit best? Choreograph the basic elements of your play or sketch.

Step 4: Take the sequence you have outlined above and set the dialogue. Use the ideas expressed in Step 1. Go back over the audio or video tape for inspiration. Don't be afraid to change, throw out, ask questions, challenge, that's part of the game and the fun—there are no right or wrong answers. Once you have a dialogue that feels right to you, set the blocking. Give everyone a copy of the script.

Step 5: Rehearse! Carry through to the dress rehearsal and final performance. You may want to discuss with your audience the process you went through to create this piece. How did your improvisations help make your expression more passionate? more creative? more meaningful?

An Alternative: You could create a monologue in much the same way. In Step 1, each person improvs a monologue from a certain point of view. Go through the appropriate steps to improve and edit the monologues for a performance.

Morph Tool # 56

MORPH A MUSIC TAPE

Design an original tape for a specific reason. Some examples include:

✳   a tape to use as background while studying

✳   a relaxation tape for someone under stress

✳   a tape of nature sounds to give to someone who has moved to a big city

✳   a "white noise" tape of repetitive sounds to block out noises when trying to sleep

✳   a tape of original songs and lyrics to play on the radio about a critical issue

Research: Find out what you will need to do or to know in order to make your tape. List below:

_____

_____

_____

Reflect: Think about what you will put into your tape, what messages you want to convey, and how this tape will help you morph your issue. List ideas:

_____

_____

_____

Design: Consider how you will create your tape. What special, personal touches will you add to: the sequence of your ideas and sounds on the tape; the tape jacket; the distribution of your tape, if for a large audience. List some below:

_____

_____

_____

After you or others use your tape for a period of time consider how the tape works to support your original intent. How has the tape helped morph the issue? How has it morphed you? others?

Morphing Projects
Visual and Performing Arts

1 **Making your art work for want you want!**
Hold an art fair with all the art that resulted from your morphing the issues you chose as a class or a school. You can sell or auction your art as a fund-raiser for school or classroom. Or money from the ticket sales of your performance could be used for critical identified issues, such as helping a homeless shelter. Or perhaps you could use the money to take a special field trip? Or the money could go towards a trip to visit the president to let him know what you think about a certain issue. Use the money gained to support a passion! Design a full action plan with what you would do. You could even document every step of your action plan with a photo essay or video documentary and then show it to the people who bought your artwork. They'll love it!

2 **Write a Sacred Song.**
Songs can catapult change. They bring unity to diversity. Think of the songs that spoke of the people's pains and rallied the people to do something, such as the black spirituals during the Civil War or the songs of Bob Dylan during the 60's. In ancient mythologies and teachings the sacred songs of nations stirred deep memory and brought wisdom to the people. Create a sacred song that will act as an agent of transformation toward our future destiny.

* Consider fundamental teachings of all times and all cultures, such as love, respect, humility, patience when writing your lyrics.

* Decide what your main message will be. Listen to a variety of songs from different cultures—Native American, African, Tibetan, Chinese—for ideas and inspiration.

* You can also create ancient musical instruments, such as drums, flutes, rattles, for accompaniment.

As a class you could write lines in your song which reflect individual ancestry and unify diversity by morphing it into one sacred song! Sing your song for the student body and for parents in a special performance. Discuss the process of creating this song, and how this song reflects your hope for the future. Record your song and get it on local radio stations.

Morphing Projects
Continuation Visual and Performing Arts

3 **Make a library come alive.**
Each student in the class decides who he or she will be. Some great writer or thinker of the past or present such as Albert Einstein, Anne Frank, Gloria Steinam, or Col. William Powell. After you have chosen your critical issue to morph, read a book or essay written by the person you have chosen "to be." While reading, think about how this great person would morph the issue at hand. Then design a play, skit, or monologue from you character's perspective, telling how to morph the critical issue for the next millennium.

4 **Design a mandala.**
Research the concept of a mandala. What is it? What is it used for? How can certain shapes convey distinct messages? Then design a mandala that will express symbolically your morph of a critical issue. For instance, if you are morphing stress, draw a mandala which will have a relaxing effect on those who look at it. You can draw or paint a two–dimensional one or create a 3–D mandala from string, yarn, wire, or beads.

Use the following evaluation forms to give
feedback on the morphing process.

Send in your completed forms to

ꟿORPHING OF AMERICA.

13601 Ventura Bvd., Suite 227
Sherman Oaks, CA 91423
www.morphamerica.org

140

Teacher Evaluation

What did you find most valuable about this process?

_____

_____

_____

_____

On a scale of 1–5 (5 being the highest) rate the following:

_____ level of student involvement

_____ effectiveness of the curriculum materials provided

_____ effectiveness of the morphing process

_____ your level of participation

_____ overall effectiveness of the entire program

What changes would you make in the morphing process in the future to better meet the needs of your students?

_____

_____

_____

_____

Will you repeat a morphing process with your students? Why or why not?

_____

_____

_____

_____

_____

_____

Student Evaluation

What was your opinion on the chosen subject that you morphed when you first started?

_____

_____

_____

What shifts did you feel during this process of this opinion?

_____

_____

_____

After completing your Morphing of America Project, how have you changed your feelings or opinions on the subject?

_____

_____

_____

How have you changed as a result of participating in this process?

_____

_____

_____

How was this different than your regular school work?

_____

_____

_____

Would you want to do this again? Why or why not?

_____

_____

142 School Administrator Evaluation

On a scale of 1–5 (with 5 being the highest) rate the following:

_____ Perceived success of the Morphing of America Project by your teachers

_____ Perceived success of the Morphing of America Project by your students

_____ Level of student involvement

_____ Level of teacher involvement

_____ Level of your involvement

Would you like your school or district to participate in another Morphing of America Project? Why or why not?

_____

_____

_____

_____

_____

_____

_____

_____

_____

_____

_____

_____

_____

_____

_____

_____

ADDITIONAL RESOURCES AVAILABLE

www.merrieway.com   www.peacesmarts.com

BOOKS BY MERRIE LYNN ROSS

Bounce Off The Walls- Land On Your Feet

Life As An Improv' – HAHA Healers Series

Happy Heart Journal

Adventures of Funny Mummy

Peace Smarts Curriculum

Morph America Curriculum

Morph America 2 – Community

Nartikki – Soul Dancer

Courses/Workshops/DVD's

The Bully Solution- Peace Smarts – DVD, course materials.

Peace Smarts Within E-Course with MP3's /mini book

HAHA Healers Teleseminar, E-Course, Live Workshops

Life As An Improv'-E-course, MP3's + Bonus Teleseminar.

Merrie Lynn is available for media interviews, live events, lecture and motivational speaker engagements, Tele-seminars, and workshops.

ABOUT THE AUTHORS

Merrie Lynn Ross – multi award winning filmmaker/author/actor has starred in 35+ TV/films. Best known as daytime's first comedienne, she giggled into millions of viewer's hearts on 'General Hospital'. Internationally acclaimed as a child advocate, honored by President Clinton, she created "Morph America" and "Peace Smarts" curriculums, helping over two million families to create a culture of peace.

Gloria DeGaetano, M. Ed – is an educator with over 35 years experience – as a curriculum specialist, classroom teacher, University instructor, and public schools administrator. Currently as a teachers trainer she consults with school districts nationwide. Ms. DeGaetano has written several books including Media Smarts 4 Young Folks and Screen Smarts: A Family Guide to Media Literacy.

Enjoy this FREE Gift!

BYRON`S SERIES BE REAL, LAUGH & LOVE

BE Real
Laugh & Love

BE Real, Laugh & Love's Inspirational content
will be sent to you with instructions. An amazing way into
your heart's desire and how to actualize your truth.

Go to: www.bereallaughlove.com

MediaMorphUs - publisher
www.merrieway.com